LEIBNIZ
LOGIC AND METAPHYSICS

Video plerosque, qui Mathematicis doctrinis delectantur, a Metaphysicis abhorrere, quod in illis lucem, in his tenebras animadvertant.

De primae philosophiae emendatione, et de notione substantiae. Acta Eruditorum Lipsiensia 1694, pp. 110–12

Leibniz
Logic and Metaphysics

by

GOTTFRIED MARTIN

Translated from the German by

K. J. NORTHCOTT

AND

P. G. LUCAS

BARNES & NOBLE, Inc.
NEW YORK
PUBLISHERS & BOOKSELLERS SINCE 1873

B
2598
.M273

CONTENTS

PART ONE—LOGIC

v

CONTENTS

PART TWO—METAPHYSICS

PREFACE

To present a complete exposition of Leibniz's philosophy would be to solve a problem to which he himself did not know the answer. The author can only hope that this work may find readers who subscribe to the words which Leibniz wrote to Gabriel Wagner: 'I, for my part, think little of refutation but much of exposition, and when I receive a new book, I try to see what I can learn from it and not what there is to criticise in it.'

It would be impossible to write a book on Leibniz without receiving a great deal of help. I have to thank the university libraries of Bonn and Mainz for their constant assistance. I wish to thank my publisher, Herr Albert Pick, for his unfailing support; and in particular I should like to thank my assistant, Herr Heinkamp, without whose expert and indefatigable help this book could never have been completed.

GOTTFRIED MARTIN

ABBREVIATIONS

References to Leibniz's works are given in the text using the following abbreviations:

GM   *Leibnizens mathematische Schriften*, ed. C. I. Gerhardt, Berlin, 1849 ff.

GP   *Die philosophischen Schriften von G. W. Leibniz*, ed. C. I. Gerhardt, Berlin, 1875 ff.

E   G. W. Leibniz, *Opera philosophica, quae extant latina, gallica, germanica omnia*, ed. J. E. Erdmann, Berlin, 1840

Ak.   G. W. Leibniz, *Sämtliche Schriften und Briefe*, ed. by the Prussian Academy of Sciences, Darmstadt, 1923 ff.

PART ONE

LOGIC

CHAPTER I

THE DOCTRINE OF PRINCIPLES

§ I. CONFLICTING JUDGEMENTS ON LEIBNIZ'S LOGIC

To the Romans, Janus, the two-headed god who looked both into the past and the future, symbolised fateful military decisions. He might also be regarded as a symbol of intellectual decisions, for these too look as much to the past as to the future. Leibniz's two most important objectives, logic and metaphysics, have this Janus-like character. As a first approximation, his metaphysics is more closely connected with the past, with philosophical tradition, while his logic looks decisively into the future. This is specially true if, like Leibniz, we regard logic and mathematics as forming one entity, but even within this entity the Janus character appears again. Leibniz preserves most carefully his connection with traditional logic, yet it is in logic that he anticipates the future with genius.

Leibniz's logic has long been the subject of careful study and a great diversity of judgement exists about it. Perhaps the greatest discrepancy is found between Heinrich Scholz and Bertrand Russell. In his lecture to the Prussian Academy of Sciences[1] Scholz praises Leibniz as the founder of an incontrovertibly secure system of logic and mathematics. Russell entitled his work *A Critical Exposition of the Philosophy of Leibniz*.[2] It might have been better to call it 'A critical exposition of the contradictions in the philosophy of Leibniz'. Even though the positive and enthusiastic voices in support of Leibniz are more numerous than the negative and sceptical ones, nevertheless this contradiction is frequently encountered.

Such judgements depend on both systematic and historical considerations. Systematically they depend on whether the critic considers a completely secure and precise foundation for logic to be possible at all. Historically it may be asked what Leibniz contributed to providing such a foundation for logic and mathematics, and further what Leibniz himself thought of the possibilities of such a foundation and what he thought of his own achievement.

Scholz's attitude is unambiguous, and could hardly be more extreme.

'The construction of such a metaphysic, in Leibniz's sense, must reach a level of precision such as mathematics itself has not achieved. This level of precision is essential if such a system of metaphysics is to provide a reliable foundation for the logic of the leading deductive sciences. This system of metaphysics must then be so thoroughly constructed that it can itself be made the object of a mathematical theory. But then it must have been raised to a level of precision substantially higher than that of mathematics; in other words, it must be of metamathematical precision' (p. 231).

Leibniz is the prophet of the study of the foundations of logic and mathematics (p. 221)—even though he could not accomplish what he demanded.

'The human spirit on the level of precision which Leibniz demanded is not a phantom but a form of the spirit which can be mastered; for it has been achieved, and what is real must also be possible. . . . We must know what we want. We must know what we demand from the scholar and from scholarship. It seems to me that I am not mistaken if I expect the scholar and scholarship to help me in every possible way to stand securely upon *terra firma*. It is certain, in any case, that this is what Leibniz demanded of the scholar and of scholarship. For this reason I declare myself on his side and on the side of the fundamental research which satisfies this demand of his' (p. 242).

Scholz can justifiably appeal to Leibniz for support for his own optimism, but whether such far-reaching optimism is objectively justified is certainly difficult to determine. If we look at the present state of research into the foundations of logic we are inclined to caution. There is in existence an unencompassable variety of views and opinions, and Heinrich Scholz was himself unable to carry out his programme completely.

Bertrand Russell arrives at a completely different conclusion. He is constantly pointing out the contradictions in Leibniz. The general thesis of Leibniz's logic, 'the predicate inheres in the subject', is regarded by Russell as problematical and contradictory, and he is probably not completely wrong in this view. He can then come to the sceptical conclusion:

'The Universal Characteristic, therefore, though in Mathematics it was an idea of the highest importance, showed in philosophy a radical misconception, encouraged by the syllogism, and based upon the belief in the analytic nature of necessary truth' (p. 171).

It is true that Russell's book on Leibniz is one of his earliest works. It appeared first in 1900 and Russell took back some things that he had said earlier in a preface to the new edition published in 1937. Nevertheless, he apparently maintains his original judgement in principle.

This astonishing discrepancy between Scholz and Russell makes a new investigation of Leibniz's logic desirable.[3]

§ 2. THE PRINCIPLE OF CONTRADICTION

The principles of contradiction and of sufficient reason are placed by Leibniz at the beginning of all knowledge and frequently mentioned together. In the *Theodicy* § 44, he says:

'In order to understand this point better we must remember that there are two main grounds for our rational conclusions; that of contradiction, which states that of two contradictory sentences the one is true the other false, and that of the determining reason, according to which nothing happens without reason or without a determining cause' (GP VI, 127).

Leibniz speaks in the same sense in the second letter to Clarke.

'The great foundation of mathematics is the principle of contradiction, or identity, that is, that a proposition cannot be true and false at the same time; and that therefore A is A and cannot be not A. This single principle is sufficient to demonstrate every part of arithmetic and geometry, that is, all mathematical principles. But, in order to proceed from mathematics to natural philosophy, another principle is requisite, as I have observed in my *Theodicy*: I mean, the principle of sufficient reason, viz., that nothing happens without a reason why it should be so, rather than otherwise.'

Leibniz frequently refers to these principles. They are mentioned together in the *Monadology* § 31, 32, and the principle of contradiction is very fully discussed in the *Nouveaux Essais* I, 1, 4 and 10 (GP V, 68 and 78).

Leibniz regards the principle of contradiction and identity as one and the same. In his correspondence with Clarke he uses the expression 'the principle of contradiction or of identity'. Aristotle, who was the first to discuss the principle, asserted that it has both a logical and an ontological significance. It may, perhaps, be said that we stress the principle of being when we speak of the principle of identity, whilst we are concerned primarily with the principle of knowledge if we speak of the principle of contradiction.

Leibniz is fond of expressing the principle in colloquial language, for example in § 44 of the *Theodicy*. The expression used in the second letter to Clarke has the more symbolic form 'A = A'. We also find the symbolic language in the *Addenda ad specimen calculi universalis*: 'a is a' and 'a is not non-a' (GP VII, 224). Couturat gives other examples of the symbolic representation of the principle.[4]

Initially, the principle of identity affirms the constancy of an ontological determination. Animal is animal, and in the negative form, animal is not non-animal (*Addenda*, GP VII, 224). A square is not a circle, sweet is not bitter (*Nouveaux Essais* I, 1, 18; GP V, 59). The proposition could be paraphrased as: everything which exists and is real is bound to maintain its being and its reality and its determinations, so that it preserves them identically.

If we describe our principle as the principle of contradiction, we are primarily considering its logical meaning. It is then a statement about propositions and states, as for example in the *Theodicy* I, 44, that of two contradictory propositions, one must be true and the other false.

Leibniz sees an immediate connection between the ontological and the epistemological significance of the principle: something real cannot simultaneously be itself and its opposite, something real cannot embrace a characteristic and its opposite. A square must be a square and cannot simultaneously be a circle, a square must have four sides and cannot simultaneously have five sides. As a result, the corresponding propositions are either true or false:

'A square is a square, a square is a circle, a square is not a circle.'
The ontological determination which is called for by the principle
of identity expresses itself in the cognitive determination which is
called for by the principle of contradiction. To say that reality is
expressed in true and false propositions and, conversely, that true
and false propositions represent reality, is to say that this principle
is a principle of being and of cognition.

We may now enquire after the sources and grounds of the principle of contradiction, and because this is a first principle we shall
doubtless encounter difficulties. Leibniz answers, with complete
certainty, that this principle, like all other *a priori* truths, is innate.

The *Nouveaux Essais* are devoted particularly to the exposition
of this doctrine. This work takes the form of an argument with
Locke: Leibniz had prepared it for the press, but his letter to
Remond de Montmort of 20 August 1714 (GP III, 612) shows that
he held up publication when he heard of Locke's death. The
Nouveaux Essais were first published by Raspe in 1765 and one of
its first enthusiastic readers may well have been the forty-one-
year-old Kant.

Locke considers that all knowledge stems from experience and
for this reason a dispute with Locke was the right place for Leibniz to expound the opposite thesis: that reason draws all pure
knowledge from itself, that all pure knowledge is inborn. To these
possessions which reason carries within itself belong all the necessary truths, particularly the truths of logic, arithmetic, and geometry (*Nouveaux Essais* I, 1, 5; GP V, 73). Leibniz draws our
attention to Plato, who, using a slave as an example, demonstrates
in the *Meno* that we all possess mathematical knowledge, though
it is true that Plato assumes an original experience through the pre-
existence of the soul. Leibniz will not even admit the validity of
this, as it assumes some sort of experience; he simply maintains
that our soul has always contained innate truths and innate ideas.

This naturally leads us, as Leibniz clearly shows, to the question,
what is the meaning of 'contain'? What do we mean when we say
that our soul has always 'contained' innate ideas?

First, we do not mean that our soul always thinks innate truths,
that it is always aware of them. We know a great deal of which

we are not thinking at a given moment, of which we have to re-mind ourselves if we wish to think of it now. It is true that this is knowledge which we have gained through experience at one time or another, and which we have to call to mind. If we regard earlier experience as pure, then we take Plato's viewpoint, if empirical, then Locke's.

Leibniz rejects both points of view. The soul draws pure ex-periences only from within itself. Perhaps this is most clear in the case of pure concepts, which are innate ideas. We ourselves are a being and for this reason alone are able to draw from within our-selves the pure concept of being. For this reason alone we can dis-cover it as an innate idea. 'And I should very much like to know how we could have the idea of being if we were not beings our-selves and did not thus find being within ourselves' (*Nouveaux Essais* I, 1, 23; GP V, 71). The same holds good for the concepts of unity, difference, substance, and all other pure concepts (I, 3, 18 and Preface; GP V, 96 and 45).[5] Similarly, we have within us the pure concepts of numbers and all the valid truths about them (I, 1, 23).

The statement that we have these innate truths within us means, therefore, that our soul can draw these concepts and truths en-tirely from within itself without giving any heed to external experience.

A distinction can be made in the case of necessary truths, which in their totality are innate truths, by observing that certain truths can be demonstrated from other truths. This is true, as a rule, for mathematical truths as such. Other truths, on the other hand, cannot be demonstrated. Identical propositions, which we shall discuss in Chapter II, belong to this category, together with the principles. Above all, the principle of contradiction is an innate truth, which we find within ourselves.

The obligatory nature of our principle becomes especially clear if we consider God's thought. The question of whether the prin-ciple of contradiction also holds good for divine thought was one which was frequently discussed in the Middle Ages. Augustine and Thomas Aquinas affirm that it does, whilst other thinkers fear that God's omnipotence would be unduly limited if it were sub-jected to any laws, even the principle of contradiction.

In the *Theodicy*, Leibniz argues at length against such an opinion. Bayle expressed it in the following words which are quoted in full by Leibniz:

'In so far as there are propositions, which are eternally true because of their own nature and not because of divine ordination, which are not true by virtue of a free decision of His will, but rather are recognised by Him as being necessarily true, because their nature demands it . . .' (*Theodicy* § 190; GP VI, 229).

The antithetical suggestion would mean that God had determined all truths as an act of His free omnipotence. God has willed that three times three equals nine when He might just as easily have willed that three times three should equal ten (§ 187). Bayle reports this as an opinion of Descartes and some of his school (§ 185). Leibniz rejects this thesis in one of the few passages in which he resorts to irony.

'Is it really possible that the joy of casting doubt upon everything should give a clever man such pleasure that he should hope and wish to believe that two contradictory things are never found together merely because God has forbidden it, when he could just as easily have commanded that they should always be together? Therein lies a beautiful paradox' (*Theodicy* § 185; GP VI, 227).

This recourse to divine thought once more reveals the dual nature of the principle as both ontological and epistemological. The world was created by God: this is one of Leibniz's principles to which we shall frequently refer. All true propositions exist as having been thought, primarily, by God. God, however, thinks nothing which is contradictory, and God creates nothing which is in contradiction to itself or to the other works of God.

This principle, which is at once the principle of contradiction and the principle of identity, is valid for the essence of God as well as for the essence of his works, for God's thought as well as for our own. We discover this principle and the truth of it when we reflect upon ourselves. Leibniz sums up in this way:

'. . . and very often the consideration of the nature of things is nothing other than the knowledge of the nature of our spirit and of those innate ideas, which it is completely unnecessary to seek outside. Thus I call those truths innate which only need that consideration to be verified' (*Nouveaux Essais* I, 1, 21; GP V, 70).

This wording suggests that there is some consideration by which innate ideas, and thus the principle of contradiction, can be verified. It would have been very desirable for Leibniz himself to have clarified the method of such a consideration or at least to have given a detailed and concrete exposition of it. Leibniz really seems to have considered the principle of contradiction to be so self-evident that as far as he was concerned any verification was quite unnecessary.

§ 3. THE PRINCIPLE OF SUFFICIENT REASON

'(The principle of sufficient reason) according to which nothing happens without a cause or a determining reason; that is, without something by which one can explain *a priori* why something is present rather than not present, why it is thus and not completely otherwise. This great principle is present in all things and no example can ever be cited to contradict it' (*Theodicy* § 44; GP V, 127).

'However, as I have observed in my *Theodicy*, in order to proceed from mathematics to physics, a further principle is necessary, namely the principle of sufficient reason: that is, that nothing happens without there being a reason for its happening thus and not differently' (2nd letter to Clarke; GP VII, 355).

'. . . and that of sufficient reason, by virtue of which we consider that no fact can be true or exist, no statement can be true, unless there is a sufficient reason why it should be thus and not otherwise. Even though these reasons can most often not be known by us' (*Monadology* § 32; GP VI, 612).

There are numerous other passages in which the principle occurs, particularly in the vast quantity of posthumous works. On principle, however, we prefer to quote evidence from those works which Leibniz himself published, bearing in mind that the *Monadology*, the *Nouveaux Essais* and the correspondence with Clarke, though not actually made public during his lifetime, may be regarded as having been prepared for publication by Leibniz.

There is an instructive example of the application of the principle in the second letter to Clarke:

'For this reason Archimedes in his work on balance, found it necessary when proceeding from mathematics to physics to employ a particular case of the principle of sufficient reason. He takes it as agreed that a balance will remain in a state of equilibrium when everything is divided equally between the two sides and the same weights are applied to the ends of the arms. For there is, in this case, no reason why one side rather than the other should fall' (GP VII, 356).

This example must have been of interest to Leibniz for a number of reasons. First of all he found it valuable that Archimedes should already have stated and applied the principle in the special case of the balance. Secondly, this example shows clearly how mechanical processes are unequivocally determined by this principle. It is true that we ourselves, like Leibniz, are immediately interested in the mechanical process as a whole but it is easy to extend Archimedes' argument. The law of causation then appears as a special case of the universal principle of sufficient reason.

The principle of sufficient reason also applies to human behaviour and especially to historical events. An example which Leibniz was fond of quoting is one which is also frequently mentioned by classical philosophers: If I go out of a room, I must either first place my left foot or my right foot over the threshold. This seems to be quite fortuitous and is, moreover, subject to my free will. However, according to Leibniz, the principle of sufficient reason also holds good here. I place my right foot first upon the threshold when, and only when, there is sufficient reason for me to place the right foot and not the left foot first (*Theodicy* § 46; GP VI, 128).

Another much discussed case is that of Buridan's ass. This wretched animal stands between two bundles of hay, which are exactly similar and which also appear to the ass exactly similar. Leibniz describes the ass as standing between two meadows and being drawn as much to the one as to the other (*Theodicy* § 49; GP VI, 129). According to the classical argument, the animal will die of hunger since it cannot decide which bundle of hay to choose.

This is precisely Leibniz's view. According to the principle of sufficient reason there must be a reason for the ass to choose the right-hand bundle rather than the left. If there is no such reason, then it will choose neither bundle, just as Archimedes' balance will not move without sufficient reason, and the wretched animal will be sacrificed to principles and die of hunger. So far so good, but according to Leibniz, the situation cannot arise in this form. The two bundles of hay can only appear equal to the animal if in fact they are identical; this in its turn assumes that their environment and all the attendant factors, such as wind, are themselves identical. This again could only be true if the world were completely symmetrical with regard to a plane passing through the middle of the ass. However, such a construction of the world would of itself violate the principle of sufficient reason. The case of Buridan's ass is, then, conceivable in terms of the principle, but cannot be realised because of the consequences of the principle (Letter to Coste of 19 December 1707; GP III, 402).

In the field of logic we find another application of the principle. Every true proposition must have a reason for being true. The logical significance of the principle is brought out in a number of places of which perhaps the most pregnant is a letter to Arnauld of June/July 1686 quoted by Russell. Leibniz is here speaking of both principles and formulates that of sufficient reason in the following way:

'. . . that nothing is without reason, or that every truth has its proof *a priori*, drawn from the notion of the terms, although it is not always in our power to arrive at this analysis' (GP II, 62).

The logical interpretation of the principle raises a problem of the relationship of the two principles to which we shall return later.

Finally, the principle of sufficient reason also turns out to be valid for divine thought and action. There were people who, while willing to recognise the validity of the principle of contradiction for divine thought, hesitated to subject God's actions to the necessity expressed in the principle of sufficient reason. There are good grounds for this. Leibniz, however, reveals here again his ever-characteristic consistency of thought, a characteristic of which he is himself well aware. Thus he says in the *Theodicy* § 44, for example, of the principle of sufficient reason:

'It will suffer no exception whatsoever, otherwise its strength would be weakened, for nothing stands on weaker foundations than those doctrinal edifices in which everything wavers and is riddled with exceptions. Mine is not subject to this error for in mine everything obeys universal laws which at the most only restrict each other' (GP VI, 127).

Divine action also is no exception and must be determined by the principle of sufficient reason. God never acts arbitrarily, but always for good reasons, and these reasons rest in God's only desiring what is best and only being able to desire what is best (*Theodicy* § 200 and letter to Coste of 19 December 1707; GP VI, 235 and III, 402).

Physical, philosophical and theological questions are all bound up in the problems of the principle of sufficient reason. This web of problems is completely characteristic of Leibniz and is perhaps most clearly expressed in his correspondence with Clarke, a London clergyman. The correspondence begins with a letter from Leibniz in 1715 and consists of five letters and answers to them: his death prevented him from answering Clarke's last letter. Clarke was a close friend of Newton and it could therefore be assumed from the first that the correspondence was closely connected with him as well. Documentation now available confirms this.[6] Leibniz himself also saw it in this light, for he writes to J. Bernoulli on 7 July 1716 of a correspondence 'with Newton or what comes to the same thing, with his Hyperaspita Clarke' (GM III, 963). In accordance with contemporary practice, the correspondence was intended for publication and Leibniz himself prepared an edition which was presumably held up by his death. After Leibniz's death, Clarke published the correspondence without further delay in 1717 in *A Collection of Papers*. This correspondence may, therefore, be included among the works which Leibniz had completed for publication.

In the correspondence a number of questions arise which were then regarded as physical, but would today be looked upon as cosmological. How long has the world existed? Has it been in existence an infinite number of years or was it created a finite number of years ago? What is the spatial extent of the world? Does the world occupy infinite space into infinity or is it a finite island in infinite space? What of atoms? Does matter fill space continuously or does it consist of atoms which are of finite size and are separated by finite distances in space? The two great founders of modern mathematics and physics hold opposing points of view. Leibniz teaches the infinite duration and the infinite extent of the world and the continuous diffusion of matter, while Newton (and Clarke with him) teaches the creation of the world a finite number of years ago, the finite extent of the world and the atomic structure of matter. They are, however, both agreed that the final solution of these problems can only be reached on the basis that God created the world. Thus Leibniz writes in the postscript to the fourth letter:

'To omit many other arguments against a vacuum and atoms, I shall here mention those which I ground upon God's perfection, and upon the necessity of a sufficient reason. I lay it down as a principle, that every perfection, which God could impart to things without derogating from their other perfections, has actually been imparted to them.'

To this Clarke responds with the opposite thesis:

'But they who believe that God created matter in what quantity, and at what particular time and in what particular spaces he pleased, are here under no difficulty. For the wisdom of God may have very good reasons for creating this world, at that particular time he did.'

On the other hand, the creation of the world a finite number of years ago would mean for Leibniz that in an empty and thus completely homogeneous infinite period of time, a particular moment was distinguished by the creation of the world, but as there cannot be a sufficient reason for such a moment of creation it is an impossible assumption.

This shows clearly that Leibniz not only holds that the principle of sufficient reason is valid for divine thought and action but also for all states and attributes of the world.

The problem of a justification of the principle of sufficient reason raises two possibilities. There can be no doubt that, like all *a priori* principles, the principle of sufficient reason was for Leibniz an innate truth, yet some innate truths, among them almost all logical and mathematical propositions, can be demonstrated from other truths. Is this also true of the principle of sufficient reason? If this principle could be proved, clearly it could only be proved by the principle of contradiction. Does it correspond exactly to this principle in being a completely independent principle which cannot be proved?

These two possibilities were considered very early but we still lack an acceptable solution. The whole question was a constant source of dispute in the eighteenth century both among Leibniz's disciples and his opponents. Christian Wolff holds that the principle is demonstrable and gives a proof of it in his *Ontology* of 1736, § 70. A. G. Baumgarten reproduces this proof in a somewhat attenuated form in his *Manual of Metaphysics*, a work which served as the basis of Kant's lectures and is reprinted in the Academy edition of Kant's works (Vol. XVII, p. 31). However, doubt was soon cast upon this proof and Crusius regards it as wrong and sees the principle of sufficient reason as indeducible (*Entwurf der notwendigen Vernunftwahrheiten*, 2nd edn., 1753, § 31).

The problem exercised Kant throughout the whole of his life. In the *Nova Dilucidatio* (I, 391 ff.), written in 1765, he rejects Baumgarten's and Wolff's proof and substitutes a new one, which later, however, he no longer regarded as valid.

In the *Critique of Pure Reason* Kant looks upon the principle of sufficient reason as being identical, for all practical purposes, with the principle of causality. As he does not present any logical proof of the principles but gives a transcendental authentication, it could be said, in the Leibnizian sense, that the principle of sufficient reason is not proved but verified. Kant regards the difference between analytic and synthetic propositions as fundamental. Analytic propositions can be proved simply by the principle of contradiction, synthetic propositions cannot be proved in this way. It is in this light that Leibniz's often repeated differentiation between the two principles interests Kant. The principle of sufficient reason goes beyond the principle of contradiction and becomes an independent principle of cognition, and so gives the first hint of synthetic propositions. This means that all proofs based on the principle are of necessity false, as Kant states in an important passage in the *Critique of Pure Reason*:

'for lack of this method, and owing to the erroneous assumption that synthetic propositions, which the empirical employment of the understanding recommends as being its principles, may be proved dogmatically, the attempt has, time and again, been made, though always vainly, to obtain a proof of the principle of sufficient reason' (A 217, B 264).

In a late work generally known as the polemic against Eberhard, Kant sums up his relationship to Leibniz, first analysing the proof of the principle given by Eberhard and then sharply criticising the false steps in the proof (VIII, 193–8). Finally, at the end of this short work he expresses his attitude to Leibniz in terms of the principle of sufficient reason:

'Is it credible that when Leibniz set so much store by his principle of sufficient reason as a new addition to the philosophy that had existed up to his time, he wanted it to be understood as objective (as a natural law)? It is so well known and (within the appropriate limits) so abundantly clear, that the most stupid person could not think it a new discovery; and on this it was indeed exposed to the scorn of several antagonists who did not understand it. Leibniz saw the principle as a purely subjective one, that is to say, as a principle which was only connected with a critique of pure reason. For what does he mean when he says that there must be other principles beyond the principle of contradiction? It is as much as to say that only those things which lie within the concepts of the object can be understood according to the principle of contradiction; if anything more is to be said of them then something must be added and this addition will have to be a principle which is distinct from the principle of contradiction, that is to say, it must have its own separate reason. Today, at least, we call this last type of proposition synthetic and Leibniz merely wished to say that in addition to the principle of contradiction (as the principle of analytic judgements), there must be another principle, the principle of synthetic judgements. This was certainly a new and noteworthy suggestion for a fresh line of inquiry in metaphysics; one which was in fact begun a short time ago'[7] (VIII, 247 ff.)

It is true that Kant is here basing his observations very firmly upon his own system of concepts but he is manifestly attempting, with good grounds, to establish a genuine connection with Leibniz.

The problem of whether the principle of sufficient reason can be proved from the principle of contradiction or whether it is a completely independent principle has not yet been resolved.

Bertrand Russell, however, seems to have inaugurated a method of solving the problem which promises to be successful. He divides the problem into two parts. On the one hand two different types of proposition are distinguished by the two principles. The principle of contradiction constitutes the necessary truths of logic and mathematics, while the principle of sufficient reason characterises contingent truths. Such a relationship, however, between the principle of sufficient reason and contingent truths is to some extent in contradiction with the logical significance of the principle. Russell tries to resolve this difficulty by speaking of two meanings of the principle of sufficient reason:

'This connection . . . gives the essence of the law of sufficient reason as applied to actual existents. At the same time, we shall see that the law has also a wider meaning, in which it applies to possible existents as well. The confusion of these two has rendered the connection of the law with the principles of contradiction very difficult to understand. The distinction will, I think, enable us to clear up the connection between Leibniz's two principles' (p. 35).

There is however very little support to be found in the text for this notion of a dual meaning. I think it is best if we develop Russell's thought and speak not of a dual meaning but of a dual function of the principle of sufficient reason. It is, in fact, possible to see two different functions of the principle, in mathematics on the one hand and in physics on the other. The principle is valid for both of those sciences. All true propositions—in mathematics as well as in physics—have their reason. In mathematics, however, the function of the principle is to characterise mathematical propositions: it is not required for the deduction of individual mathematical propositions. In physics it has a different function. Here Leibniz found it necessary to use the principle of sufficient reason in order to deduce a whole series of propositions. We have seen examples of the use of the principle for the proof of statements about physical phenomena in the correspondence with Clarke. While it characterises both mathematical and physical propositions, it is not used to prove mathematical propositions whereas there are a number of physical propositions which could not be proved without it. This view finds support in the text. In his second letter to Clarke, Leibniz says: 'In order to proceed from mathematics to natural philosophy another principle is requisite.' He then goes on to say that Archimedes had need of this principle in order to prove a physical thesis. We may assume that this dual function of the principle is the cause of certain vacillations in Leibniz's work and that it has, in consequence, helped to give rise to the diversity of interpretations which exist.[8]

§ 4. POSSIBILITY AND NECESSITY

Leibniz deals exhaustively with the problems of modality in the *Theodicy*. This is the only philosophical work, apart from some youthful writings, which was published by Leibniz himself. He must have been working on it for a long time, since although it appeared in 1710 we know that it was nearly complete in 1707. It is scarcely possible to imagine the impact which this work made upon the eighteenth century; it was probably the most widely-read book of the century, at least in Germany, and is in a sense the embodiment of the Enlightenment. If today it is neglected in nearly everything written about Leibniz this is probably not only because Leibniz was intent upon a comprehensible, even popular, presentation of his material, but also more probably because the work contains a number of very long-winded passages. I consider this neglect of the *Theodicy* unjustified.

In Part II, § 168, Leibniz says that he is concerned with the nature of the possible and the necessary. He begins by discussing things which never happen. As an example Bayle had cited 'the Grand Mogul is going hunting tomorrow'. If we consider the opposite statement, 'the Grand Mogul is not going hunting tomorrow', we see that only one of these events can happen. We may then ask, is one of these propositions true now today, and its opposite false? One of them must be true and the other false. The question is whether it has already been determined which of them is true and which false. If the proposition has already been determined today, then tomorrow's happening is also determined and we have lost our freedom of choice. If, on the other hand, it has not already been determined which of the statements is true we seem to be faced with a violation of the principle of contradiction which demands that of two contradictory statements the one must be true and the other false (*Theodicy* § 169; GP VI, 211).

Epicurus, following Aristotle, assumed that future happenings of this sort are not determined and so the statements which treat of these happenings are not subject to the principle of contradiction. Aristotle discusses the problem in *de Interpretatione* (19a, 26f). The passage has, however, always been variously interpreted and has recently attracted renewed interest from the point of view of multivalued logic,[9] but there is still no agreement upon the correct interpretation of it. Epicurus, and Aristotle if interpreted in this way, see the two happenings as both possible happenings: go hunting or not go hunting. The opposite view is that only what is going to happen is possible and therefore what has never happened (having regard to the total cosmic process) can never have been possible. This is the doctrine of the Stoics and in this connection Bayle mentions Arrian, Chrysippus, Cleanthes, Archidemus and Antipater (*Theodicy* § 170). Theologically this means that God can only do what he actually does and this is what Peter Abelard taught, though his doctrine was rejected (§ 171). Spinoza is also to be included with this party (§ 173).

In his own discussion of the problem, Leibniz with some justification starts by saying that this is to a large extent merely a verbal quibble. We can define possibility quite easily in Chrysippus's terms; a happening is then only possible when all the conditions have been fulfilled. For an event which does not happen all the conditions (*omnia rei non futuræ requisita*) have never been completely present (§ 172). In recent times Nicolai Hartmann has also defined possibility in this way.[10]

Leibniz then takes up Bayle's definition: the impossible is that which contains a contradiction within itself. The corollary to this is that the possible is that which does not contain a contradiction. 'Everything which implies contradiction is impossible, and everything which does not imply contradiction is possible' (§ 173). This fundamental definition is found in so many passages in the published as well as the unpublished works that there is no need to quote any more.

This definition of the possible now yields a definition of possible worlds. At the end of the *Theodicy* (§ 413) there is a very graphic example. Sextus has complained of his fate to Jupiter, who commands him to go to Athens. Here Pallas Athene takes him into a palace which contains innumerable rooms, in each of which a cosmos is displayed, in other words, a possible world. Sextus sees a world in which he goes to Corinth where he buys a garden in which he finds a treasure so great that he can spend the rest of his life as a wealthy and respected man. He sees another world in which he goes to Thrace, where he marries the daughter of the king and succeeds to his throne. All these different possible worlds point to one: the best and the actual. Leibniz understands a possible world as the complete history of a cosmos and two cosmic courses differ in respect of an infinite number of happenings, even if they are only required to differ in one. Possible worlds differ, too, in the good which they contain, and one of them must contain a maximun of good. That is to say that there must be a sufficient reason for God to realise one of the many possible worlds. This sufficient reason can only be that one of the infinite number of possible worlds must be the best, and this is the reason why God created this world and only this one (*Theodicy* § 8 and § 416).

Corresponding to this distinction between the actual and the merely possible worlds there is the distinction between the two types of truth:

'There are two types of truth, those of reason and those of fact.

Truths of reason are necessary . . . and their opposite is impossible, truths of fact are contingent and their opposite is possible' (*Monadology* § 33; GP VI, 612).

This distinction between rational and factual truths is fundamental for Leibniz. Logical and mathematical truths are rational truths. As their contradictory opposites contain a contradiction, they are valid in every possible world. In every possible world, therefore, the three-dimensional truths of Euclidian geometry are valid and Leibniz chooses the idea of three-dimensionality as an example of rational truth (*Theodicy* § 351). On the other hand, factual truths are not valid in all possible worlds, so that for every factual truth there is at least one possible world in which it is not valid.

Expressing this thesis in terms of the theory of modality, we may say that in the field of rational truth every necessary and possible circumstance is also simultaneously necessary and actual. In Nicolai Hartmann's terms, possibility, reality and necessity are all mutually implied in rational truth.

Leibniz avoids the use of the term 'reality' in the sense of purely mathematical reality. In Leibniz's terms, therefore, we can only say: in the field of rational truth, possibility and necessity mutually imply each other. In the field of factual truth, however, every possibility is far from being real and even further from being necessary. At the same time, the facts of the actual world are in some sense necessary. The world cannot be different as it would be contradictory to God's goodness to create any other but the best of all possible worlds. In order to give an account of this necessity, Leibniz distinguished between two types of necessity: logical or metaphysical necessity which concerns those circumstances which cannot be otherwise, because their opposite contains a contradiction, and physical or moral necessity which concerns those circumstances which could have been different according to the principle of necessity, but which are determined by the principle of sufficient reason. We can therefore now say: in the field of rational truth the possible is at the same time logically or metaphysically necessary while in the field of factual truth the real is physically or morally necessary. In the field of rational truth, possibility and logical necessity are mutually implied; in the field of factual truth reality and physical necessity are mutually implied.

This concept of possible worlds was of great importance for Heinrich Scholz. He points out that this fundamental distinction of the real world from the totality of all possible worlds is an application of the mathematical principle of maximisation.[11] This is doubtless correct, but Scholz seems to overlook the fact that Leibniz himself pointed out the connection between the concept of the best of all possible worlds with the principle of maximisation (GP VII, 303). On the other hand another of Scholz's lines of thought seems to have certain inherent difficulties. He discusses principles valid in every possible world, including worlds which contain only one thing or only two things.[12] It seems to me difficult to decide whether a world which contains only one thing represents a possible world for Leibniz. Such a world would violate a number of fundamental principles, for example the principle of continuity. Nor can we see how the possibility of such a world could be consistent with the doctrine of monads. On the other hand, such a world would only be impossible if it contained a contradiction within itself, but it is by no means obvious, at least at first sight, that a world which contains only one thing would of itself be contradictory. The question is a difficult one and I have not found any passage in Leibniz's works which would appear to give a definite answer.

CHAPTER II

THE DOCTRINE OF CONCEPTS, JUDGEMENT AND INFERENCE

§5. THE CONCEPT

THE doctrine of the concept is the origin of all Leibniz's logic, but it is also the source of all the difficulties. He starts from the observation that our concepts are as a rule compound. Thus the definition of 'homo' shows that it is a compound concept, and that it can be split up into two partial concepts, animal and rational. The question immediately arises as to whether this division can continue indefinitely or whether, after a finite number of steps, we shall ultimately arrive at certain fundamental concepts which are no longer divisible. Leibniz, unheedful of all the difficulties, always regarded the second solution as the necessary one. His letter to Vagetius of 2 December 1679 shows how much he was exercised by the problem:

'In the matter of simple concepts or of those which are conceived in themselves, I have often thought that, although I consider it very difficult for such to be adequately expressed by men, we can consider them by acting as if we were able to express them. It may first be asked whether any of them are true simples or whether there is really a subdivision *ad infinitum*, as in other divisions (for it seems as if nothing at all can be conceived if nothing is conceived in itself) and, further, whether there is a single one rather than many. If there is a single one how can so many compound notions spring from it? If many they will, of necessity, have certain things in common, such as possibility, just as they will have certain relations among themselves. Otherwise they could not claim to constitute compound notions. How then are these same notions simple? Thus, whichever way we turn we encounter difficulties. However, the solution of these questions is of great importance for the determination of the true principles of knowledge' (Academy edition, II, I, 497).

We are faced with four tasks if we assume the existence of

simple, fundamental concepts: (1) analysis of compound concepts into their component parts; (2) synthesis of concepts into compound concepts, starting where possible from simple concepts; (3) complete representation of the simple, fundamental concepts; (4) complete representation of compound concepts.

The best exposition of the concept is probably contained in the *Meditationes de cognitione, veritate et ideis* which appeared in the *Acta Eruditorum* in 1684. Any concept which presents itself to us is, generally, a compound one, a *notio composita*. Leibniz gives the following examples: gold, weight, colour, aqua fortis, chiliogon, number, form. These compound concepts are based on simple ones, *notio primitiva, irresolubilis, indefinibilis*. At this point we are faced with the demand for the analysis of these concepts into unanalysable fundamental ones, but it is doubtful whether such an analysis is possible: 'I do not know whether it is possible to give a perfect example of this.' Leibniz mentions numbers as being, at least, relatively simple concepts (GP IV, 423).

If the simple concepts were to be completely given by a completed analysis, then synthesis would be reduced to a mere system of combinations. Leibniz conceived very early the idea of such a combinatorial system of conceptual composition and it is developed fully in the *De arte combinatoria* which was published in 1666 when Leibniz was twenty years old. He gives a clear statement of the structure of analysis:

'Analysis is as follows: (1) any given term may be resolved into formal parts or its definition may be given; these parts may be resolved again into parts, or the definition of the terms of the definition, until we finally reach simple parts or indefinable terms' (GP IV, 64).

This procedure corresponds exactly to that of the *Meditationes* (1684); definition in particular is concerned with the reduction of compound concepts to their constituent parts. The necessity of simple concepts is justified with a reference to Aristotle. If we assume complete analysis and synthesis in this way it is possible to obtain systematically the totality of all true statements: 'Thus when these things have been confirmed it is possible to discover all subjects and predicates . . .'

Leibniz gives two examples: Let us assume, he says, that there are four simple, fundamental concepts, and let them be represented by the numbers, 3, 6, 7, 9 (in this early work he does not employ the obvious idea of using prime numbers). The products of pairs, triples, etc., of these numbers will symbolise the possible conceptual compounds and it can easily be seen that compounds of the most diverse sort are possible (GP IV, 65).

Leibniz draws his second example from the foundations of mathematics. He gives a table of 27 fundamental concepts and suggests twenty-four classes of differing grades of composition. Among these compound concepts we find, for example, quantity, straight line and diameter. Essentially this is a classification of the known mathematical definitions. He does not try to give a complete picture and in fact his table of 27 fundamental concepts does not consist of really fundamental or simple and no longer compound concepts. Leibniz maintains that the analysis could be completed, but for the moment, he says, he has no time. 'By this method we could develop all the definitions in the *Elements* of Euclid—if there were sufficient time' (GP IV, 70). It is to be feared that even with plenty of time Leibniz would have been unable to complete this task.

This doctrine of the composition of concepts seems to appear in all Leibniz's works. In the *Monadology* § 33, he says:

'When a truth is necessary, it is possible to find the reason for it by analysis, resolving it into ideas and truths which grow simpler and simpler until the fundamental ones are reached.'

Logical questions play a somewhat less important part in the *Theodicy*, although we still find a number of passages where the doctrine of compound concepts is indicated, for example in § 99 of the *Causa Dei*: 'Innate light consists of non-complex ideas, then of developing and, finally of complex ones.' The problem is, understandably, of considerable importance in the *Nouveaux Essais*, where Chapters 30–32 of Book II are expressly concerned with it. Here, too, Leibniz talks of simple and compound ideas. He is concerned, in particular, with the question of what rules govern thought in the composition of ideas (GP V, 109, 156, 245, 275).

It is hardly possible even to estimate the importance of the problem in the unpublished works and I should like to draw attention to Couturat's two books.[13] It seems as though even Couturat has not exhausted the material which is to be found in the manuscripts for he only gives a table of contents for some important works.

Historically, the analysis of a concept into its constituent parts was a fundamental problem for Greek thought. In Greek mathematics, medicine and in the sophists we find the first attempts to arrive at definitions. Aristotle tells us that Socrates was looking for definitions and the early Platonic dialogues show that he employed the analytic method. In the works of Plato the process culminates in what has been called Plato's pyramid of concepts. The most comprehensive examples are to be found at the beginning of the Sophist (219D), where first the angler and then the sophist himself are defined by this process. The problem widens as Aristotle develops logic into an independent discipline. Leibniz's specific interest is the combinatorial approach, and here there is a close connection with Raymond Lull. In his De parte combinatoria, Leibniz refers to particular works of Lullus and to commentaries on them (GP IV, 61 and 74). Lull had a number of disciples whom Leibniz referred to as Lullists; in a broader sense, Gassendi, Giordano Bruno, Hobbes and Tholanus are also regarded as his followers. Leibniz was also interested in contemporary studies by Kircher. The historical connections of the combinatorial procedure have been investigated by several authors including Couturat.[14]

Autobiographical reminiscences show that Leibniz was concerned with this problem from a very early age, a fact which could be inferred from the comparatively systematic exposition in the De arte combinatoria. Leibniz tells us that he became acquainted with the Aristotelian doctrine of categories when he was very young and that he at once busied himself with the problem of establishing the totality of all possible predicates and so the totality of all true propositions, by means of the combinatorial juxtaposition of the categories, which he conceived as simple fundamental concepts. Leibniz must have been twelve or thirteen years old at the time (GP VII, 516). We may ignore the question of whether the application of combinatorial thought to Aristotelian logic sprang independently from the young Leibniz's very lively talent for combination, later to be confirmed by his reading of the works of Raymond Lull or of works influenced by him, or whether the initial inspiration came from these works. The play of spontaneity and receptivity, discovery and confirmation cannot be resolved, particularly in the case of so versatile a mind as Leibniz.

The combinatorial theory of concepts has its difficulties. The distinction between simple and compound concepts must involve an analogous distinction between different faculties of knowledge and this is, in fact, the problem with which the *Meditationes* are concerned (GP IV, 422). Access to compound concepts is a faculty of discursive thought. This holds good even for numbers. On the other hand, simple fundamental concepts can provide no basis for discursive thought and must be comprehended by pure intuition.

'The cognition of a fundamental, distinct notion can only be achieved intuitively, just as the thought of compound, multiple ones is purely symbolic' (GP IV, 423).

However clear this distinction may appear, it is full of difficulties. Leibniz attacks the Cartesian doctrine of *perceptio clara et distincta* in the *Meditationes*. His criticism is that there is no criterion for the presence of such a perception. This is true, but Leibniz is open to the same reproach. He, too, gives no criterion as to when a perception is intuitive and moreover he gives no criterion as to when a compound is no longer composite but simple.

In these circumstances it is understandable that Leibniz should consistently avoid the obvious question as to the number and type of fundamental concepts. The approach would be more convincing if one could at least gain some clue as to what the table of fundamental concepts might look like. It is true that Leibniz made experiments along these lines but he seems, justifiably, to have found them unsatisfactory. Presumably the concept of the *ens* would have to be regarded as the first of the fundamental concepts. Perhaps the concept of the *unum* also belongs here, or is, at the very least, closely related.

It is not even possible to be clear as to whether Leibniz regarded the number of fundamental concepts as finite or infinite. In a letter of October 1671 to Duke Johann Friedrich concerned with obtaining his post in Hanover, Leibniz surveys the discoveries which he has made up to that time.

'In philosophy I have discovered a method of achieving in all sciences, by means of the *ars combinatoria*, what Descartes and others have achieved in arithmetic and geometry by algebra and analysis. This *ars* was first developed by Lull and P. Kircher but they were far from recognising all its potentialities. By its means all notions in the world can be reduced to a few simple terms which serve as an alphabet and by using combinations of this alphabet a means will be found to discover systematically all things together with their theorems and whatever can be found out about them. This invention, in so far as God willing it may be put to work, is considered by me to be the mother of all inventions and to be the most important of all, even though it may not be recognised as such at the moment. I have, by its means, discovered everything that is now to be related and I hope to discover even more' (GP I, 57).

Revealing as this letter may be for Leibniz's optimism it contains little that is concrete. When he says that there are only a few fundamental concepts, he is expressing himself in the most cautious terms. What are we to understand by this statement? Leibniz compares fundamental concepts with the letters of the alphabet both here and elsewhere, so we must assume that the number of concepts is finite. In other places he compares them with prime numbers, the products of which can produce all other numbers,[15] yet such a comparison leads us to postulate an infinite number of fundamental concepts. The obvious question as to the number of fundamental concepts must presumably be left unanswered.

Every fundamental concept must express a positive reality and two fundamental concepts can never contradict one another. This must follow from the fact that fundamental concepts cannot contain any compound elements. For a fundamental concept to express the negation of a reality it would have to contain a negative, but this is impossible if the concept is not compound. For the same reason, two fundamental concepts cannot contradict one another. A contradiction implies that the same content will be both affirmed and denied, so that as long as there can be no negation there can be no contradiction. In this way fundamental concepts are closely related to an old theological and philosophical concept, the concept of the attributes of God, the *attributa Dei*. In the *Réflexions sur l'essay de l'entendement humain de Mr. Locke*, which was written for publication in 1696, but not published until 1708, Leibniz refers to the *Meditationes* of 1684 and writes: 'But fundamental ideas are those of which the possibility cannot be demonstrated, and which are, in effect, nothing but the attributes of God' (GP V 15). This connection with the attributes of God serves to confirm our view, since God's attributes are positive realities and can never contradict one another.[16]

There are many obscurities and difficulties about fundamental concepts. In the case of compound concepts things are somewhat clearer, but here different difficulties arise. The general criterion of possibility now becomes the criterion for the existence of concepts. Anything which contains a contradiction is impossible, anything which contains no contradiction is possible. As a result, all compounds of concepts which contain a contradiction are impossible, and conversely all compounds are possible which contain no contradiction. Leibniz makes the same distinction between true and false concepts and gives the following definition:

'It is obvious which ideas are true, they are those in which the notion is possible, the false ones involve a contradiction' (GP IV, 425).

Here Leibniz is clearly departing from tradition, which permits the nominal definition of each and every concept and then proceeds to seek a decision as to whether the object designated by this nominal definition exists or not. Thus it is possible to define the concept of a regular seven-faced object, but it is subsequently revealed that such an object cannot exist. Leibniz, on the other hand, regards such a concept as a *notio impossibilis*. This concept does not exist, therefore it cannot, strictly speaking, be given by a nominal definition: the definition of a regular seven-faced object is merely a verbal juxtaposition.

Leibniz's approach makes it necessary to demonstrate the lack of contradiction in all concepts. We shall investigate this problem

in Chapter V; for the moment, we shall content ourselves with
stating it. There are a number of concepts which do not, at first
sight, appear at all suspect, but which are seen upon closer in-
spection to be contradictory.

Leibniz demonstrates this by a series of examples, and for this
purpose he frequently employs the concept of the highest speed.
It can be demonstrated by a thought experiment (conducted
naturally under the assumptions of classical mechanics) that the
concept of the highest speed is contradictory (GP IV, 424). The
same is true of the concept of the greatest number, which is also
contradictory.

It was soon clear to Leibniz that these difficulties arise from the
concept of totality and the related concepts of maxima and
minima. This is what he has in mind when he writes to Oldenburg
from Paris on 28 December 1675:

'I posit the possibility of such a being, or of any idea corresponding to
these words, hence it follows such a being exists. We seem to think
many things (confusedly if you like) which imply a contradiction, for
example the number of all numbers. The notion of infinity ought to be
highly suspect to us, and the notion of minima and maxima, of the
most perfect and of totality itself' (GM I, 85).

These difficulties also apply to Descartes' proof of the existence
of God. In the *Meditationes* he points out that the concept of God
in this proof is defined as a maximal concept, the most perfect
being or a being a greater than which cannot be contemplated, a
being which embraces all perfections. It would not be an *a priori*
impossibility that this concept of totality should be contradictory
in itself. It is, in fact, true that Leibniz was convinced that this was
not the case; the concept of God defined in this manner is not
contradictory. But the lack of contradiction in a proof of the
existence of God must be demonstrated. Until these conditions
are fulfilled, says Leibniz, referring to Thomas Aquinas, then the
proof derived from the most perfect being (*ens perfectissimum*)
cannot be considered valid (GP IV, 424).

Two further objections may be raised against the combinatorial
theory of concepts. The first objection would be that, in this
theory, concepts can only unite in one single way, that is by logical

addition. The old standard formula is *Homo = animal rationale*, and Leibniz allowed himself to be guided by this traditional example. In reality it was completely clear to him that by no means all definitions could be constructed in this form. In the case of the definition of natural numbers, for example, Leibniz saw that the old rule: *Definitio fit per genus proximum et differentiam specificam* (A definition is made by the nearest type and a specific difference) was not enough, and that natural numbers must rather be defined by a chain definition: 2 = 1 plus 1, 3 = 2 plus 1, etc. (GP V, 393). In the *De arte combinatoria* there is logical addition, which Leibniz indicates by a point, but he also recognises that other forms of combination are required for the familiar mathematical definitions (GP IV, 72).

Leibniz's analytic theory of judgement which we shall discuss in the next section leads to another difficulty. According to the theory of judgement, a concept B can only be predicated of a concept A if the concept B is contained in the concept A as part of it. On this basis nothing at all can be said about a fundamental concept—neither possibility, nor simplicity, nor compatibility. Such a fundamental concept of which no other concept can be predicated seems of itself to be impossible. Plato showed in the *Parmenides* the difficulties which arise if the concept of the ἕν is accepted as a fundamental concept in this sense. Leibniz himself saw these difficulties, though with his knowledge of Plato this is hardly surprising. He writes in the letter to Vagetius quoted above: 'In what way, then, are these notions simple? No matter in which direction we turn, we encounter difficulties.'

We shall meet similar difficulties in the analytic theory of judgement, and there is, it seems to me, only one explanation for the difficulties in this and in the combinatorial theory of concepts: both theories were conceived by Leibniz so early, that they cannot be reconciled with his later discoveries and understanding.

§6 JUDGEMENT

The analytic theory of judgement follows quite consistently upon the combinatorial theory of concepts. The term analytic does not occur in the narrower sense of analytic judgement in Leibniz's work, but only in the wider sense which springs from the opposition analysis/synthesis. However, as the term has been introduced and is used by Couturat and Russell,[17] it may be worthwhile retaining it.

The investigation of Leibniz's analytic theory of judgement may begin with the concept of identical propositions.

'The primitive truths of reason are those which I call by the general name, identical, since it seems that they only repeat the same thing, without teaching us anything. They are either affirmative or negative. The affirmative ones are as follows: Everything is what it is, and in any number of examples A is A, B is B. I shall be what I shall be, I have written what I have written.

>   Et rien en vers comme en prose,
>   C'est estre rien ou peu de chose.

An equilateral rectangle is a rectangle' (*Nouveaux Essais* IV, 2, 1; GP V, 343).

In the *Monadology* § 35, Leibniz mentions 'Identical statements the opposites to which contain an express contradiction'.

Identical judgements can be divided into two classes, absolutely identical, and virtually identical. An example of an absolutely identical judgement would be: a triangle is a triangle, or A is A. The example of a virtually identical proposition would be: *Homo est rationalis*, A is B. The proposition formed by substitution: *animal rationale est rationale*, or AB is B, could then, depending on one's point of view, be regarded as an absolutely or a virtually identical judgement. This distinction occurs in many passages. In the *Addenda ad specimen calculi universalis* the first two classes of propositions which are true in themselves are the following:

'1. a is a, Animal est animal.'
'2. ab is a, Animal rationale est animal' (GP VII, 224).

The idea is further developed in another unpublished work.

'ab is a   or (every) rational animal is an animal.'
'ab is b   or (every) rational animal is rational.'
'a is a   or (every) animal is animal' (GP VII, 218).

In yet another unpublished work we find the term 'virtually identical':

'propositions . . . virtually identical—which, of course, can plainly be reduced by an analysis of the terms (if we substitute, for the first term, a notion which is either equivalent or included) to either formal or expressed identities' (GP VII, 300).

It is also possible to distinguish between a narrower and broader sense of the word identical, senses which Leibniz often uses indiscriminately, but which can be distinguished with a little care. Leibniz can then proceed from the broader meaning of the term 'identical proposition' to the theory that all true judgements (at first he restricts this to rational judgements) are identical.[18]

We thus have three types of identical judgement, which we can represent by the three examples: animal is animal, rational animal is rational, man is rational.

In terms of the theory of concepts, Leibniz makes the generalisation: 'in every true judgement the predicate is contained in the subject.' Both Couturat and Russell have paid particular attention to this thesis, which is found in the study just mentioned.

'Thus as in any proposition: A is B (if B is truly predicated of A), thus B is contained in A, or the idea of it is contained in some fashion in the idea of A' (GP VII, 300).

Couturat's references are presumably fairly complete; the most succinct is perhaps the following:

'Therefore the predicate is always contained in the subject, either as an antecedent or as a consequence, and this constitutes the whole nature of truth in general.'

This statement that in every true judgement the concept of the predicate is contained in the concept of the subject constitutes Leibniz's analytic theory of judgement. It would be dangerous to speak of a general analytic theory of judgement, since the concept of analytic judgement is used today in a number of senses which generally differ from the sense in which Leibniz used it. On the other hand, Kant's concept of analytic judgement can be said to coincide with that of Leibniz.

'The predicate B belongs to the subject A as something which is (covertly) contained in this concept A.... Analytic judgements (affirmative) are therefore those in which the connection of the predicate with the subject is thought through identity' (*Critique of Pure Reason*, A6/B10).

If we consider the relation of Leibniz's analytic theory of judgement to his combinatorial theory of concepts, we can see that the theory of concepts is the basic theory because concepts provide the foundation for judgements. Concepts and their relations are what actually exist. Concepts and their compounds are the primary logical actuality. In a judgement this composition is only rendered explicit by making a compound concept into a subject concept and a partial concept contained in the subject into the predicative concept. Leibniz's approach is by no means self-evident. It may well be asked which, logically, comes first, the concept or the statement which forms the judgement. We can transform the question into a purely linguistic one, and ask which comes first, the word or the sentence, and from this it can be seen that Leibniz's decision is a very far-reaching one.

The analytic theory of judgement related at first to rational truths, truths of reason. Later, Leibniz extended it to cover factual truths, so that this theory of judgement applied to all true statements. The old distinction between the classes of truth now occurs in this form: in rational truths the subject concepts are compounded of a finite number of partial concepts, whilst in factual truths concepts occur which are compounded of an infinite number of partial concepts. This distinction with its consequences for the theory of science will be discussed in Chapter V. It is of no consequence for the theory that the predicate is contained in the subject whether that subject contains a finite or an infinite number of partial concepts.

The analytic theory of judgement is the centre of both Couturat's and Russell's accounts, but is assessed very differently by them.

Couturat regards the theory as the foundation-stone of Leibniz's philosophy:

'We have thus been led to discover that his logic is not only the heart and soul of his system, but also the centre of his intellectual activity and the source of all his inventions, and we also recognise in it the obscure or, at least, hidden hearth from which sprang so many luminous "fulgurations" ' (*Logique*, p. xii).

Couturat's thesis is by no means as clear on examination as this brilliant statement would lead us to believe. In what sense does the whole of Leibniz's philosophy spring from his theory of judgement? Does Couturat intend this to be taken historically? Does he wish to suggest that the theory of judgement came first and that everything else, and particularly the doctrine of monads, developed from this theory? I have been unable to discover any attempt by him to trace such a development in Leibniz's philosophy. Or does he intend his thesis to be regarded systematically? Are we to say that all statements on Leibnizian philosophy can be deduced from the theory of judgement? It can certainly not be denied that the analytic theory of judgement, and the combinatorial theory of concepts upon which it is based, have a fundamental importance and that they reach, for example, deep into the doctrine of· monads, but the thesis goes much further than this. The concept of *representatio*, for example, is fundamental to the theory of monads, but it seems doubtful whether this concept can be deduced from Leibniz's theory of judgement.

Bertrand Russell rejects the theory of analytic judgement. He demands that an account of a philosopher should not be restricted to the historical. 'But in addition to the purely historical purpose, the present work is designed also, if possible, to throw light on the truth or falsity of Leibniz's opinions.' We completely agree with this demand. In philosophy every work, that purports to do more than prepare the material, must pose the question of truth. It must show what the author has stated, but it should also if possible show which of the author's statements are true and which false.

Russell's discussion of the analytic theory of judgement is to be found in the first three chapters of his book. In the first chapter Russell develops five premises of Leibniz's philosophy: The first is that every proposition has a subject and a predicate. In the second chapter Russell describes the analytic judgement. 'Every proposition is ultimately reducible to one which attributes a predicate to a subject. In any such proposition . . . the predicate is somehow contained in the subject.' The subject is defined by its predicates and would be a different subject if these were different. A judgement which has such properties is described by Russell as analytic. In other words, the predicate forms part of the idea of the subject. (The part omitted from the quotation refers to existential propositions and we shall return to this later.) Two further important statements are made in the same chapter: 'An analytic judgement is one in which the predicate is contained in the subject' and 'The subject is an agglomeration of attributes of which the predicate is a part.'

Russell analyses this theory of judgement and shows that it is based upon the assumption that every subject has or does not have a predicate. 'This is', says Russell, 'a very ancient and very respectable doctrine.' This analysis is without doubt correct and is supported by the fact that Leibniz himself represents judgement in a general fashion by the formula: A is B, or AB is B. Russell then asks two questions: 'Are all propositions reducible to the subject-predicate form? Are there any analytic propositions and if so, are these fundamental and alone necessary?'

The first question, whether all judgements are of the form A is B, must be answered in the negative, as far as relational and existential judgements are concerned. Neither judgement can be reduced to the form that a predicate is predicated of a subject and therefore neither judgement can be an analytic judgement in Leibniz's sense.

For proof, Russell points primarily to mathematical existential judgements. The judgement 'There are three men' cannot be put into the subject–predicate form. There is here no subject which can contain a predicate, a partial concept. If we wish to use the concept of subject, then we could at best speak of three subjects. The same is true of judgements such as 'L is greater than M', 'L is equal to M', 'L is less than M'. It cannot be said of the proposition 'L is equal to M' that L is the subject or that M is the subject. If we wish to talk of subjects in this case, we have to say that there are two subjects, L and M, and that a twofold relationship between these two subjects is expressed. This is already evident in the normal mathematical form, when we write $A = B$; and is even clearer if we write the expression more correctly: $= (A,B)$. It was this relation which Leibniz discussed in his fourth letter to Clarke. Russell's interpretation of this passage is infelicitous, since he confuses ontological and logical problems, a point to which we shall return in the second half of this work.

It goes against the grain to criticise a mathematician like Leibniz on the basis of judgements of relation. It is evident that Leibniz recognised the significance of the judgement of relation, and it is equally evident that he took a lot of pains to elucidate the question. It is a troublesome problem and Russell has adopted the only possible course. We can only resign ourselves to the conclusion that on the one hand relational judgements were extremely important for Leibniz, but that on the other hand his analytic theory of judgement does not hold for relational judgements.

The second objection arises out of existential judgements, and here I am in complete agreement with Russell. An existential judgement cannot be expressed in the form: a predicate is predicated of a subject, as in this case we should have to regard existence as a predicate, which in the proper sense it is not. As Russell says, 'Existence, alone among predicates, is not contained in the notion of subjects which exist.'

Russell goes on to say in the third chapter of his book: 'Existence is thus unique among predicates. All other predicates are contained in the notion of the subject, and may be asserted of it in a purely analytic judgement. The assertion of existence, alone among predicates, is synthetic.' If this is to be regarded as an historical exposition I find it unsatisfactory to assume synthetic judgements in Leibniz, and to interpret Leibniz's opinion in such a way as to suggest that he regarded existential judgements as synthetic and not analytic. This is, as Russell admits, in contradiction to what we find in the text. There can be no doubt that, in his analysis of the proof of God, Leibniz regards the existence of God in the usual sense as a predicate, and Russell points out such a passage. Nor does the excursus on *cogito ergo sum* in the *Nouveaux Essais* provide a final decision. We can only admit that Leibniz vacillated on this question and that he regarded existential judgements when they relate to contingent things just as he regarded all judgements relating to contingent things, as being non-analytic.

Whatever is the truth of the purely historical question, existential judgements are an argument against Leibniz's analytic theory of judgement, since they cannot be expressed in the logical form A is B, simply because, as far as existence is concerned, the circumstance of a certain subject having a particular property is lacking.

Thus both relational and existential judgements are weighty arguments against the generality claimed by Leibniz's theory of analytic judgement. We shall develop a further objection in Chapter V, but we can say at this point that Leibniz's thesis 'therefore the predicate is always contained in the subject—and this constitutes the general nature of truth', cannot possibly hold good with this degree of generality.

§ 7. INFERENCE

Traditional logic is essentially the logic of the syllogism and relies primarily upon Aristotle's *Prior Analytic*. Recent studies have shown that some medieval philosophers went far beyond this, but the syllogism played a dominant part in teaching and thus in the general consciousness of the Middle Ages.

The best evidence of Leibniz's attitude to syllogistic logic is his letter of 1696 to Gabriel Wagner (GP VII, 516 f). Although not published until 1838, this letter can be supported by so many passages in other works that there can be no doubt that it truly represents Leibniz's own view, and that this view was well-known during his lifetime.

Leibniz begins by distinguishing between a logic which is the art of judgement and a logic which is the art of invention.

'By logic or the art of thinking, I understand the art of using the intelligence, that is, not merely judging what is presented but also of finding out what is hidden.'

Somewhat later he says:

'Up to now I have spoken of that part of known logic which serves discovery, now we must also think of that part which belongs to judgement.'

We regard logic essentially as the art of judgement. Of this Leibniz says:

'I must confess that all existing systems of logic are scarcely a shadow of that which I wish for, and which I see as from afar. However, to speak the truth and to give credit where it is due, I must confess that there is much that is good and useful in existing logic, to which I also am very grateful, since I can, I think, truthfully say, that even the logic that is taught in the schools has borne me much fruit.'

This is an opinion which Leibniz often expresses: one must respect Aristotle's syllogistic logic, but it is only a beginning, it must be further developed. Here Leibniz disagrees with Kant, who stated in his *Critique of Pure Reason* (B VIII) that logic was a complete system and thus had not been able to progress at all since Aristotle's time. Later developments have shown Leibniz to be right and modern logic, which has become a constantly developing science, regards Leibniz in this respect as its model.

In the letter to Wagner we find the revealing autobiographical reminiscences quoted above; Leibniz learned logic young, at the age of thirteen at the latest. He was particularly attracted by the doctrine of categories which he at once saw as a general combinatorial system.

Leibniz states his view of Aristotelian syllogistic logic as follows:

'It is indeed no small achievement that Aristotle combined these forms into an infallible rule, and was at the same time the first to write mathematically outside the science of Mathematics. I have also contributed something curious in shewing that each of the four figures has only six valid forms and thus (contrary to the common doctrine) one has as many as the other: nature is regular in all things. And this seems to me no less worthy of note than the number of regular bodies' (GP VII, 519).

Couturat has expounded Leibniz's logic in such a comprehensive and well-founded manner that I can confine myself to a short résumé. The first question concerns the number of valid inferences. The classical scheme, which derives from Aristotle and

Galen's extension, reckons a total of nineteen inferences. In the *De arte combinatoria* Leibniz had increased their number to twenty-four (GP IV, 46). However, the young Leibniz's view is hardly significant since all the additional inferences are empty ones.

The second question concerns the derivation of the second, third, and fourth figures from the first, and this embraces the important question as to whether all nineteen or, as the case may be, twenty-four, inferences are independent or whether some of them are merely certain other ones in a different form. Leibniz occupied himself a great deal with this question and there is an exhaustive discussion of it in the *Nouveaux Essais* IV, 2, 1 (GP V, 344 f.): once more I would refer to Couturat.[19]

The third question is that of the truth of the rules of inference. This question can be reduced to the truth of the *modus barbara*. Is the *modus barbara* a demonstrable proposition? If so, how can it be proved? If not, what is it?

We have not found it among the principles and there is no indication that Leibniz would have placed it among them. Leibniz regards it rather as a *consequentia per se vera*

'A consequence true in itself: a is b, and b is c, therefore a is c. God is wise, who is wise is just, therefore God is just' (*Addenda*, GP VII, 224).

This must of course be understood in the light of the combinatorial theory of concepts and of the theory of analytic judgement. If we now develop the *modus barbara*. within the framework of these theories, we find that from

$$a \text{ is } b$$
$$b \text{ is } c$$
$$\therefore a \text{ is } c \quad \text{we develop first}$$

$$ab \text{ is } b$$
$$b \text{ is } c$$
$$\therefore ab \text{ is } c \quad \text{and further}$$

$$abc \text{ is } bc$$
$$bc \text{ is } c$$
$$\therefore abc \text{ is } c$$

After such an analysis Leibniz might be justified in thinking that, because of the identity-relation, the inference is self-evident, and this clarifies an observation in the *Nouveaux Essais*. On the other hand, this point of view comes close to an attempt to prove the *modus barbara* from the principle of identity.

In any case, the inferences, taking the *modus barbara* as a standard example, contain no independent truths. The *modus barbara* depends rather on compounding the concepts a, b and c in a special manner, as ab, bc and c. Inferences are not independent truths but they too, like judgements, spring from concepts and their compounds. Thus once more we see that concepts and their compounds are the real foundation of Leibniz's logic.

The letter to Wagner is very revealing on the question of the extension of Aristotle's system of syllogisms.

'It is true that this work of Aristotle's is only a beginning and like the ABC, as there are other more complex and difficult forms which can only be used after establishing with its help the primary and more simple forms; for example, the Euclidian forms of proof, in which proportions are laid down by the inverse, compound and divided ratios. Indeed even addition, multiplication or division of numbers, as these are taught in the schools of arithmetic, are forms of proof (*argumenta in forma*) and we can rely upon them, since they are proved by the force of their form. In the same way, it can be said, that the whole of a bookkeeper's reckoning is formally closed and consists of *argumenta in forma*. It is the same with algebra and many other formal proofs, which are naked and yet complete' (GP VII, 519).

Leibniz's reference to Euclid means that the inversion of the ratio $a : b = c : d$ into $b : a = d : c$ can be regarded as a purely logical form of inference. This equation of arithmetic with logical operations contains three problems. First, these further forms must be set out; secondly, the relationship of mathematics to logic must be re-assessed from this viewpoint; and thirdly the character of logic itself must be re-assessed. We shall discuss the second and third problem in Chapter V. The first problem is one which concerned Leibniz and there are numerous treatments of it in the manuscripts which have been edited and presented with great care by Couturat. In the works which Leibniz himself published, especially in the *Nouveaux Essais* (GP V, 344) and the *Theodicy* § 28

(GP VI, 67), there are also a number of references to this under-taking and to the results which he had already achieved.

These results can be divided into two groups, the first of which would include very general laws, the second the more specialised laws of the logic of relations. The commutative, associative and transitive laws would belong to the first group in all their varying applications. The commutative law is concerned first of all with the cummutativity of the combinations of concepts. '. . . it can be said with equal truth that "Homo est rational animale" and "homo est animal rationale"? '(GP VII, 525). The same idea explained by the same example also occurs in a manuscript. The law of tautology also belongs under this heading. 'The repetition of any letter in the same term is useless and it is sufficient that it should be retained once e.g. *a a seu homo homo*' (GP VII, 222). Leibniz was particularly concerned with the law of transitivity in equations. If $a = b$ and $b = c$, then $a = c$ is a well-known pro-position but Leibniz is interested in its purely logical significance (*Theodicy* § 22; GP VI, 63). In the *Nouveaux Essais* Leibniz con-siders the *modus barbara* from the point of view of the law of transitivity (IV, 17, 4; GP V, 462). The investigation of the doc-trine of the whole and the parts also belongs here and there is in existence an almost complete manuscript which Dürr has for-malised.[20] We shall return to the logic of relations later.

In his efforts to extend logic, Leibniz relies upon a large number of predecessors. He received great stimulus from his mathematics teacher, Erhard Weizel in Jena, whom he mentions in the *Theo-dicy* § 384.

He was also stimulated by Hobbes, whom he mentions in this connection in the *De arte combinatoria* (GP IV, 64). Leibniz had a special interest in attempts to elucidate the logical structure of Euclid's *Elements* and he was himself constantly making investi-gations of this kind (GM V, 183, GM I, 191).[21]

We can see here an objective connection which still persists today. The extension of logic and the continuation of logical work consists to a large extent in the task of reducing to their pure form the methods by which mathematical conclusions are reached and it is obvious that the systematic beginnings of mathematics are of particular interest for this purpose. Not only Leibniz but many philosophers of our own day, among them Frege, Peano, Russell and Whitehead, are concerned with the reduction of mathematical thought to its pure logical form.

The question of the historical connections seems to me to be still an open one. It is commonly held that the nineteenth-century logicians had to begin at the beginning and that Leibniz's logical researches were only discovered towards the end of the century, so that the newly-developed mathematical logic merely regarded his work as confirmatory. This view is all the more remarkable since the published works, particularly the *Nouveaux Essais* and the *Theodicy*, contain plenty of indications of his aims in logic. We must therefore await a new and unprejudiced examination of this question.

CHAPTER III

THE DOCTRINE OF CATEGORIES

§ 8. THE TABLE OF CATEGORIES

THE ten Aristotelian categories represent the first scholastic treatment of the problem. They are substance, quality, quantity, relation, place, time, activity, passivity, state and position. It was early realised that this table is not complete and the so-called post-predicaments were added. Outside the table there are, more or less closely connected with the categories, the modalities possibility, reality and necessity and the transcendentals, more especially unity and being.

The table of ten categories cannot be said to represent Aristotle's final and fixed doctrine.[22] In his works we find the categories in a number of different arrangements. A table of categories consisting of the first four—substance, quality, quantity and relation—may represent Aristotle's real view.

This reduction of the ten categories to the first four main categories played a large part in the original thinking of medieval philosophers, if not in the scholastic logic of the period. It can readily be seen that there must be some superfluous definitions among the later categories and Leibniz, too, became aware of this very early on. In the autobiographical reminiscences quoted above he writes:

'I began at once to notice—as far as a thirteen year old boy is capable of noticing—that there was something very important behind this. I found delight in the so-called predicaments which appeared to me to form a muster-roll of all the things in the world and I looked in all sorts of Logics to see where such general registers were best and most exhaustively to be found. I often asked myself and my fellow-pupils to what predicament and subject this or that would belong, although I did not like to see so many things completely excluded, and even I soon dropped some of the predicaments, in particular the last two, if not, indeed, the last four, since they were included in the preceding concepts or could not be shown to be useful' (GP VII, 516).

In the *de arte combinatoria*, Leibniz begins with the table of four categories.

'1. Metaphysics, and I begin at the summit, is concerned on the one hand with the *ens* and on the other, with affections of the *ens*. As, however, the affections of the natural body are not themselves bodies, so the affections of the *ens* are not *entia*. 2. There is therefore an affection (or mode) of the *ens*, either absolute, which is called Quality, or relative, as between a thing and its part, if it has one, and which is called Quantity, or relative as between one thing and another, which is called Relation; or to speak more accurately, if we regard the part as being different from the whole, then Quantity is the relation of the whole to the part. 3. It is therefore manifest that neither Quantity, Quality nor Relation are *entia*' (GP IV, 35).

This approach contains a complete ontological programme and we shall confine ourselves at first to the question of categorial analysis. Leibniz divides the totality of what exists into three classes. Something is either an *ens* in itself or a determination of being (*affectio entis, modus entis*). The *modi entis* can be further divided into three classes: Quality, Quantity and Relation. This passage also constitutes an attempt at a systematic deduction of the categories, a deduction which has often been attempted, but always in vain.

The passage is especially interesting because the number of categories is reduced from four to three, since Leibniz states that quantity must actually be regarded as a relation. Starting from the four categories, their subsequent reduction is the central theme of Leibniz's researches in categorial analysis. It will be shown that he subsumes quantity completely under the heading of relation. This reduction also affects quality (but I should prefer not to commit myself as to the length of time which elapsed before this took place) so that this too disappears. Thus, we finally reach a table of only two categories, substance and relation. Nevertheless, because of a few residual difficulties Leibniz is always hesitant on the question of quality.

The *Nouveaux Essais* present the thesis clearly:

'This division of the objects of our thoughts into substance, modes and relations is, to my mind, satisfactory. I think that qualities are merely the modifications of substances and understanding adds relation' (GP I, 132).

Here, as in the earlier work, quantity has been completely absorbed in relation. On the other hand mode, instead of being the concept which covers both quality and relation, is now contrasted with relation. By substance Leibniz probably meant monads here, by modes the thought and desire of monads, perception and appetition (*perceptio* and *appetitus*). Perception and appetition have always been difficult to fit into any scheme of categories. Whenever they have been regarded as qualities it has always been with hesitation and for want of a better place to put them. Leibniz himself sometimes describes them as qualities (*Monadology* § 8).

Leibniz may also have included among the modes a few terms which are usually regarded as transcendentals, particularly *unum* and *bonum*. The logical determination of the categories, the question of their definition and of their classification, is in general very closely associated with their ontological determination, the question of their ontological content. In the case of substance, Russell treated the two questions separately but this seems to make difficulties and we are postponing the discussion of individual questions about categorial analysis until we come to the ontological discussion of categories in Part II of this book. For example, the question of the reduction of quality can only be discussed in connection with the mechanistic conception of Nature, where not only the secondary but also the primary qualities disappear. This shows how difficult it is to construct a purely systematic account of Leibniz's philosophy. It is by no means as easy as Russell thought. It is very plausible that it should be so difficult, for otherwise Leibniz himself would certainly have given such an account of his own philosophy.

CHAPTER IV

NEW SCIENCES

§ 9. SCIENTIA INFINITI

THE concrete scientific product of Leibniz's life's work is even more difficult to describe than the rest of his work. Leibniz views all sciences as forming a single unity from the point of view both of the subject and of the scientist. His own scientific work embraces almost all the sciences known at his time, not only mathematics and physics but also the experimental sciences and the humanities: history, language and law. The reason is to be found not merely in the all-round gifts which he possessed but at least as much in his theoretical assumptions. Our task, like that of all expositors, is to break down what for Leibniz was an original unity. As we have to break it down, we shall concentrate upon those areas which are of especial philosophical interest, either for Leibniz or for us.

In mathematics there is no doubt at all that Leibniz may be accounted a genius; a fact to which the seven-volume edition of the mathematical writings, published by Gerhardt, bears witness. This edition balances, in many ways, the seven volumes of philosophical writings. It is certain that the *Akademie* edition will considerably expand this material. Thus, Leibniz has earned a well-deserved and meritorious place in the great histories of mathematics—I need only mention those of Moritz Cantor and his school. Meanwhile a number of monographs on Leibniz have appeared. I shall confine myself to the mention of Hofmann.[23]

We shall consider first the differential and integral calculus, which Leibniz liked to call the *scientia infiniti* (GM V, 382 ff.). His plan to present a systematic account of it was never carried out (GM I, 7).

The whole problem is bedevilled by the quarrel over priority, at first involving only Leibniz and Newton, though not always conducted in a particularly laudable manner, later to be continued by their disciples in a nationalistic and partisan spirit. Today the question may be regarded as settled. I am in agreement with Bertrand Russell who maintains that Newton and Leibniz discovered the infinitesimal calculus simultaneously and independently of each other.[24] Historical and theoretical reasons support this view, for they followed different paths and used different methods for their discovery.

It is hard for us now to appreciate the difficulties of gaining acceptance for the new discovery. Leibniz was specially anxious to win the agreement of Huygens, who was sceptical for a long time and only became convinced when it had been proved that the new method could solve problems which were not capable of solution by existing means. The letter of 1 September 1691 in which Huygens finally expresses his agreement will always remain an example of the true, enlightened, scholarly attitude.

'I have further considered why several of your discoveries have eluded me and I judged that this might be the effect of your new method of calculation . . . I still cannot see the light but since you and M. Bernoulli have succeeded in doing this, I conclude that you have both been led either by your new calculus or by having acquired a greater knowledge of binomials and their mutual dependence and relations. . . . You would do me a great favour, Monsieur, if you would throw a little light upon it; which you can perhaps do in a very few words' (GM II, 98).

Leibniz, as always, is less interested in the results than the methods (GM III, 100). Infinitesimal calculus offered unusual scope for this attitude. A considerable number of partial results were already known; the problem was merely to discover a general method. Leibniz regards the infinitesimal calculus as a way of solving, by means of calculation, problems which could not be solved by existing methods, in particular by Cartesian analytic geometry. Analytic geometry introduces calculation into geometry, but Descartes only applies it to certain limited problems—limitations which Leibniz had often studied (e.g. GM V, 226 ff.). The new method, however, is not subject to these limitations. It permits the representation and investigation of any given curves whatever. It is especially useful for determining the maxima and minima of curves and Leibniz also calls it the *methodus de maximis et minimis* (GM V, 220). With the new method it is possible by differentiation to find the tangent of a curve from its equation and conversely to reconstruct the curve from the equation of the tangents or from a variable related to it. It permits us to calculate the area which a curve forms with its abscissa and ordinates or with other curves. In Cartesian geometry all these problems could only be solved for certain curves and Leibniz is convinced that they are now soluble for all curves, with complete generality by pure calculation. In fact, this is very nearly true even if Leibniz over-estimated the universality of the methods which he employed.

What interests Leibniz particularly in the new method is its arithmetical nature, its character as a calculus. Every calculation, as Leibniz clearly realises, involves constructing and operating with a system of symbols. Thus the question of the usefulness of a notation will become, as we shall see, a problem which attracted Leibniz's attention not only in the special case of the infinitesimal calculus but also generally.

The symbols generally in use today for differential quotients and for integration originate from Leibniz. In their correspondence of 1696, Leibniz and J. Bernoulli agreed on how they would use these symbols (GM III, 262 f.). In the priority quarrel Leibniz justifiably claims that the symbols chosen by him are more convenient than those chosen by Newton and he discusses this point at some length in his letter to Huygens of 3 October 1690 (GM II, 49 f.). In themselves all symbols are, of course, arbitrary and everyone has the right to express himself in his own way, nevertheless they can have a greater or lesser usefulness and so should be chosen to express relationships which are inherent in the things themselves. If we consider, for example, the series of powers of x, that is x, x^2, x^3, etc., we can determine that any letter, say m, shall represent x^2 and further, that n shall represent x^3. In this case the series x, m, n . . . would represent the series x, x^2, x^3 . . . but it can be seen at once how inconvenient such a notation would be. In the series x, x^2, x^3 the symbols themselves represent the objective relationships, but the series, x, m, n, which represents the same relationships no longer demonstrates of itself the objective relations. The position is much the same in respect of the different symbols chosen by Leibniz and Newton for differential quotients. Multiple differentiation and differentiation in several variables can only be expressed conveniently in Leibniz's notation. At the same time, there are cases where Newton's notation can be more useful, and for this reason it is still preferred today for certain problems in physics. Generally speaking, however, Leibniz's notation is the more useful and this accounts for its retention in mathematics.

§ 10. ANALYSIS SITUS

The second discipline in which we are interested is the *analysis situs*. Gerhardt published three manuscripts on this in the first volume of the mathematical papers. They are

I. *Characteristica Geometrica.*
II. Concerning *analysis geometrica propria* and *calculus situs.*
III. *De analysi situs* (GM V, 141 ff.).

Leibniz gives an extensive account of *analysis situs* in his letter to Huygens of 8 September 1679. This was an important letter. First, it was intended to promote Leibniz's nomination to the Paris Academy, a nomination which he did not obtain until 1699. For this purpose Leibniz, understandably, chose a discovery which he was convinced was fundamental and he gave a carefully considered exposition of it. Secondly, this correspondence was published in 1833 when Uylenbroek brought it out in the Hague under the title *Christiani Hugenii aliorumque seculi XVII virorum celebrium exercitationes mathematicae et philosophicae* (GM II, 9). It was therefore already effective during the nineteenth century.

In his manuscript *De analysi situs* Leibniz argues on the basis that analysis up to that time had been concerned with quantity and so belonged to arithmetic rather than geometry.

'What is commonly known as mathematical analysis, is concerned with size and not with position (*situs*) and thus belongs directly and immediately to arithmetic; it is applied indirectly, however, to geometry' (GM V, 178).

Nevertheless, there is a type of analysis which is concerned not only with questions of size but also of position. The Greeks already knew of it and the ancient Greek doctrine of geometrical loci is part of *analysis situs*.

This discipline is concerned mainly with the concepts of similarity and congruence. We must, therefore, define similarity and congruence and their axioms. When this has been done we can demonstrate a whole series of propositions: equiangular triangles are similar, or the areas of two circles are in the same proportion as the squares of their diameters.

In the final paragraph Leibniz formulates the task of the new discipline:

'Henceforth this contemplation which shews us the ease of proving truths which are difficult to prove by other means, appears to us to be a new form of calculation entirely different from algebraic calculation and equally new in its operations and use of symbols. And so it seems right to call it *Analysis situs* because it explains the situs immediately and accurately, so that even figures not delineated are depicted in the mind by signs, and whatever the empirical imagination learns from figures, the calculus can derive from signs by a sure proof, with all other consequences to which the force of imagination cannot attain: hence a supplement to the imagination, and as I may say, a perfection in that which I have set out, is contained in the calculus of situs not so much for geometry but for the inventions of machines and will have a use unknown up to this moment for the descriptions themselves of the machines of nature' (GM V, 182 f.).

In an appendix to his letter to Huygens of 8 September 1679, Leibniz gives a detailed exposition of the *analysis situs*, which is essentially the same as the one in the manuscript which we have just quoted. Here, too, Leibniz begins by saying: 'I have discovered some elements of a new characteristic, quite different from algebra' (GM II, 20). Leibniz makes considerable use of the doctrine of geometrical loci. As an example of a proposition which can be demonstrated by the new calculus he gives: 'the intersection of two spheres is a circle'. It is noteworthy that here again he mentions the description and construction of machines.

Huygens remains sceptical; his immediate response was:

'I have examined carefully what you wrote me about your new characteristic, but I must tell you frankly that I do not see, from what you have told me, that you should entertain such high hopes' (GM II, 27).

But whereas Huygens, as we have seen, was later to be convinced by the differential and integral calculus, he always remained sceptical of the *analysis situs*.

The reason for this may well be that Leibniz made no further attempt to explain his new calculus to Huygens. True, he explained it to other people, but with little success (GM V, 139).

Later developments have proved Leibniz right. In the last century Grassmann raised *analysis situs* to an independent discipline. He alludes to Leibniz in the title of his book published in 1847—'Geometric Analysis allied to the geometric Characteristic, invented by Leibniz'. The further development of this discipline and its extension in our own century is astonishing.

§ 11. SCIENTIA DYNAMICA

Leibniz's researches into *scientia dynamica* are mainly concerned with those problems which today belong partly to theoretical physics and partly to the fundamentals of physics. They begin with a double publication in 1671 (GM VI, 17 ff.). The first part entitled *Hypothesis physica nova* is dedicated to the Royal Society in London; the second part entitled *Theoretica motus abstracti* is dedicated to the Academy of Science in Paris. The two parts were printed in different forms. There follows a series of papers which Gerhardt published in the sixth volume of the mathematical writings, part of which had already been published by Leibniz in periodicals. A large number of papers which Erdmann published in the collected works and which Gerhardt included in the philosophical writings also belong here. Finally the question of *scientia dynamica* is also repeatedly mentioned in his correspondence. Leibniz started a complete résumé and he himself writes of this to J. Bernoulli:

'When I was in Rome in 1689 and was having a great deal of discussion of these things with Anzout, that most erudite Frenchman who was among the founders of the Royal Academy of Sciences, I sketched out my thoughts and put them in order in a little pamphlet. In this I proved a number of things about force, absolute and directive, about the conservation of motion in the centre of gravity, and about other things not less important than these. Whilst passing through Florence, I left it to be published with a friend who is an excellent mathematician, but as the book was not completed at that time, since I had taken it back to write the ending, the publication could not follow. I had not yet completed it, partly because many new things had developed in the meantime which were worth adding, and partly because I did not wish to thrust, as it were, beautiful truths upon those things which it did not seem likely to be accepted' (GM III, 259 and VI, 281 ff.).

Gerhardt published this manuscript in the 6th volume of the mathematical works, where it occupies 233 pages.

The content of the *scientia dynamica* belongs more to the foundations of dynamics than to the part of theoretical physics that we now call dynamics. If, in his *Hypothetica*, Newton can proudly assert: 'I do not make hypotheses', we in turn may say that Leibniz is almost entirely concerned with hypotheses, hypotheses which explain the physical laws describing phenomena. We shall concern ourselves with four problems from the *dynamica*, (1) the structure of matter, (2) the movement of heavenly bodies, (3) the measurement of force, (4) *a priori* laws in physics.

As to the structure of matter, two points of view have existed ever since the Greeks first mentioned it. Matter exists in the form of atoms which are of finite size and are distributed at finite intervals in a vacuum, or alternatively matter fills space continuously. Initially, and especially during his years as a student, Leibniz probably subscribed to the Aristotelian view of the continuous distribution of matter. Afterwards he embraces the atomic theory for a short time, as witness a letter to Thomasius published in 1670 (GP I, 15), but later he returns finally and for good to the hypothesis of a continuum. In 1695 he writes in the *Journal des Savans*,

'At first after I had been freed from the yoke of Aristotle, I toyed with the idea of atoms and a vacuum' (GP IV, 478),

and again in much the same sense in the *Acta Eruditorum* in 1698,

'But a long time ago I perceived that atoms and the vacuum (the remains of a youthful prejudice) should be abandoned' (GP IV, 514).

The dispute about the structure of matter plays a leading part in the correspondence with Clarke, which is, as we have said, in effect a correspondence with Newton. The problem is also mentioned in the correspondence with Huygens, as Huygens, like Newton, is an adherent of the atomic theory (GM II, 141 ff.). Here Leibniz points out that it is an old and fundamental dispute:

'I turn to our controversy about atoms, it is so ancient and minds are so divided that I am not in the least surprised that we do not agree upon it' (GM II, 155).

Leibniz's rejection of the atomic hypothesis is never, as far as I can see, based upon the principle of contradiction. The arguments always return to the principle of sufficient reason. From this we must infer that Leibniz regarded the atomic hypothesis in itself as being free from contradiction and, knowing Leibniz's presuppositions, we could state this in the following form: God could have created a world which consisted of atoms and such worlds must, therefore, clearly be found among the possible worlds. God created the world as it is as a world which fills space continuously, according to the principle of sufficient reason. Leibniz argues along these lines in the manuscript mentioned above. Here he says (Part II, Section III, proposition 5): 'There are no perfectly inflexible bodies . . . Hence it is to be understood that atoms are not in harmony with the laws of nature' (GM VII, 491). The same is valid, too, for the opposite concept to the atom, the concept of the vacuum of which Leibniz says in proposition 22: 'A vacuum is not consistent with the laws of nature' (GM VI, 511).

However, I feel that in his correspondence with Huygens Leibniz wishes to go somewhat further. Here he seems to regard the atomic hypothesis and the continuum hypothesis as two alternative hypotheses. This attitude may partly spring from the fact that Huygens subscribes to the atomic hypothesis and Leibniz wished to meet him half-way. Yet I do not think that it is merely a question of conciliation; it seems probable that Leibniz genuinely wished to discuss this possibility in accordance with his general principles.

The second problem of *scientia dynamica* which we shall consider is the ether hypothesis. Leibniz developed this hypothesis in the *Hypothesis physica nova* which appeared in 1671 and maintained it for the rest of his life. We shall take as our basis the paper which Leibniz published under the title: *Tentamen de motuum coelestium causis* in the Acta Eruditorum of 1689.

Leibniz begins by asserting that we must start from Kepler's laws.

'Hence he (Kepler) discovered that any primary planet describes an elliptical orbit, in the second of whose foci is the sun, moving by the law that by radii leading from the sun to the planet, areas are constantly cut off proportional to time' (GM VI, 148).

The task now is to discover the reasons for Kepler's laws of motion and Leibniz expresses particular surprise that Descartes did not take this task upon himself.

'I am frequently astonished, however, that Descartes did not come to produce the reasons for Kepler's laws of motion.'

There can only be one reason for the movement of celestial bodies: space must be continuously filled with an ether. This ether is set into motion by the radiation of light from the sun and this motion of the ether transfers itself to the celestial bodies and is the reason for their movements.

'Indeed, I judge that nothing remains but that the cause of celestial movements derives from the movements of ether or as the astronomers would say from certain subsidiary spheres or fluids.'

Leibniz can therefore sum up by saying that the movement of the celestial bodies arises from the movement of the ether: 'Hence it follows that the planets are moved by the ether.' He is next concerned with deriving the details of Kepler's laws of motion from the ether hypothesis and he busies himself with this task in the continuation of the *Tentamen* as well as in parallel studies.

Leibniz constantly returned to his argument against Descartes, and in the sixth volume of the mathematical writings we find several papers on this theme. A paper published in 1686 in the

Acta Eruditorum is called '*Brevis demonstratio erroris memorabilis Cartesii at aliorum circa legem naturalem secundum quam volunt a Deo eandem semper quantitatem motus conservari, qua et in re mechanica abutuntur*' (GM VI, 117).

This title alone shows what a strong emotional conntoation this problem had for Leibniz. It is, therefore, understandable that there should be numerous contributions to this theme in the philosophical writings. The problem also plays a large part in his correspondence. That with Papin which is particularly concerned with this question was not published by Gerhardt, but much of the dispute with Papin was carried out in periodicals, and includes the article published in 1691: *De legibus naturae et vera aestimatione virium motricium contra Cartesianos responsio ad rationes a Dn. Papino mense Januarii anni 1691 in Actis Eruditorum propositas* (GM VI, 204 ff.).

The dispute hinges upon two closely related questions. The first, which is the more philosophical, is concerned with the nature of the material body, the second more physical question is concerned with the concrete measurement of forces. The first question considers whether Descartes is correct in regarding bodies as *res extensae*, by which the material body is essentially determined by mere extent, thus relying upon a fundamentally geometrical consideration. Leibniz saw early that this definition was insufficient. A body must also be determined by its force. This means, among other things, that a body cannot be determined merely by spatial moments, but that temporal moments are also involved in its fundamental structure. The connection with the *Monadology* is clear and it is understandable that this discussion should occupy a great deal of Leibniz's attention. Perhaps Leibniz's most terse formulation is in the article on the concept of substance, published in 1694.

'So that I may give some foretaste of this thing, I shall say for the meantime, that the idea of force or power, for the explanation of which I have destined the special science of dynamics, brings more light to the understanding of the true notion of matter' (GP IV, 469).

The second, physical, problem is concerned with the measurement of that dimension which is conserved whatever mechanical changes take place. Descartes determines this dimension by the product of mass and speed (mv) while Leibniz makes it the product of the mass and the square of the speed (mv^2) (GM VI, 117 and VII, 193 ff.). There can be no doubt that Leibniz's formula has a sound basis in phenomena which he has interpreted correctly, but Leibniz becomes so passionately involved in the argument that he is unable to see that his theses depend upon certain assumptions, and that there are other assumptions, which would make Descartes' statement correct. It is only necessary to consider (in terms of Newton's first law of motion) a single body moving in a straight line at a constant speed to see that in this case both in Descartes' sense, and in Leibniz's, the impulse (mv) in the one case and the kinetic energy (mv^2), in the other, remain constant.

The final question of Leibniz's dynamics which we wish to discuss is the question of whether there are *a priori* laws in physics. This has already been demonstrated by the fact that the principle of sufficient reason includes the law of causality as a special case, and hence there can be no doubt that Leibniz considers this law, within the framework of physics, as an *a priori* law. But many physical concepts which are more concrete can still be demonstrated *a priori*. The structure of matter whether considered from the viewpoint of the atomic or of the continuum theory is, fundamentally, a problem which can only be solved *a priori*. The question of constant quantity, that is of the measurement of forces, can also, according to Leibniz, be solved *a priori*.

Leibniz's writings on dynamics as a whole are concerned basically with what we should today call fundamental questions. Leibniz frequently proceeded in a highly traditional way and at least in his works on dynamics, traditional points of view are often most oddly intermingled with highly advanced ones. It therefore seems understandable that Leibniz did not himself publish the final *Dynamica de potentia et legibus naturae corporeae*. It could hardly have compared favourably with Newton's *Philosophiae naturalis principia mathematica*.

§ 12. SCIENTIA DE RELATIONIBUS

If we take a sufficiently wide view of the concept of relation we can regard the general logic with which Leibniz was concerned as a general theory of relations. Leibniz said as much himself. In an unpublished paper which Erdmann later entitled 'De scientia universali seu calculo philosophico', Leibniz says:

'In place of Euclidean axioms and theorems about size and proportion, I have found others of much greater moment and of more general use concerning coincidence, congruence, similarity, determinates, cause and effect, about force, relations in general, about containing and content' (GP VII, 199).

Coincidence, congruence, similarity and determinates are the problems of the analysis situs; cause and effect, or force, are the problems of the scientia dynamica; and relations in general, containing and content, are the problems of the new logic. It is noteworthy that the new logic appears here specifically as the science of relations in general. As the reference to Euclid shows, the whole question turns upon re-interpreting a series of axioms, rendering explicit the implicit pre-suppositions and defining exactly the concepts contained in them. In accordance with Leibniz's presuppositions about the nature of science, they must then be described in a manner which permits them to be subjected to a calculus and finally to be proved by this laborious method. We might select as a convenient example, 'If two dimensions are equal to a third, then they are equal to each other.' We shall discuss Leibniz's treatment of this proposition in § 16.

The manuscripts which Erdmann published in the philosophical writings fall within the sphere of this scientia de relationibus in universum (GP VII, 198 ff.). In addition there are the manuscripts which Gerhardt published in the philosophical writings (GP VII, 1 f.), besides those which he included among the mathematical writings under the title Initia mathematica (GM VII, 1 f.). Couturat deals with the problem of a general theory of relations in Chapter 8 of his book on Leibniz's logic.

It is Leibniz's efforts towards the establishment of a new logic which have led to his being regarded as the standard-bearer of a new discipline which has undergone a most astonishing development in the last century. It is, therefore, understandable that this logic should have been expounded by many authors who approach Leibniz from the basis of modern formal logic. I need only mention Dürr's exposition of Leibniz's works in the field of syllogism; his revision of one of Leibniz's manuscripts is also very revealing. I may also mention Yost's semantic exposition, which suffers from being written from a very narrow viewpoint. Two comprehensive treatments are already available. The first is by Heinrich Scholz and appears in his *History of Logic* and the second is by Bochenski. Both of these works contain bibliographies of specialist literature.[25]

In view of all this, it is astonishing how often the opinion is expressed that there is no historical continuity in the development of logic and that modern formal logic had to start afresh and only found confirmation in Leibniz's works after their subsequent discovery. In my view there are not enough individual monographs available to furnish evidence as to whether there is or is not historical continuity, but we know that enough of Leibniz's works had certainly been published by the beginning of the nineteenth century. The *Nouveaux Essais* appeared in 1765, the correspondence with Bernoulli was published in 1745, and there are other places as well where Leibniz speaks of his plan for the renovation and extension of logic. Historical continuity was therefore possible; and I personally believe that such a continuity actually exists and that those who were concerned with the renovation of logic in the nineteenth century were the direct descendants of Leibniz.

§ 13. CHARACTERISTICA UNIVERSALIS

As a result of successful work in a number of separate fields, of which we have only given examples, Leibniz began to consider the possibility of a *characteristica universalis*. The term *ars characteristica*, for example, is found in the paper on *De scientia universali seu calculo philosophico*:

'the progress of the art of rational discovery depends for a large part upon the perfection of the *ars characteristica*' (GP VII, 198).

The best survey appears in the manuscript *Characteristica Geometrica* which was written in 1679. Here Leibniz begins by defining the concept of the sign:

'Signs are certain things by which the inter-relationships of other things are expressed and which are easier to manage than the things themselves' (GM V, 141).

Two questions now arise, the first as to the usefulness of signs and the existence of better or worse signs and the second as to the general meaning of signs.

In this particular manuscript the first of these questions is tackled immediately:

'By the degree of greater exactitude in signs, that is to say by how many more relations they show, that much greater is their use.'

The problem is complicated by the possibility of arbitrary designations. There is no doubt that a person may designate a thing in any way he likes, but this does not exclude the possibility of having a better or worse designation for particular problems.

'It must certainly be known that the same things can be designated in different ways, and that some ways are more suitable than others.'

The best example of this is numerals:

'And no one would disagree that the characters of present-day Arabic (or Indian) numbers are more suited to calculation than the old Greek or Roman ones, even though these could be used for calculation.'

In fact numerals are the best example of this problem of signs in general. The Greeks used consecutive letters of the alphabet for the units, 1, 2, etc., for the tens, 10, 20, etc., and for the hundreds, a system which is highly unsuited to calculation and could only maintain itself because, for all practical purposes, the abacus was used for reckoning. Roman numerals are built up on a system of strokes augmented by the initial letters of some of the larger numbers. The process is, generally, an additive one though in certain cases it is subtractive, so that the following series emerges: I, II, III, IV (subtractive), V, VI, VII, VIII, IX (subtractive), X, XX, XL (subtractive), L, LX, LXX, LXXX, XC (subtractive), C, CX, etc. It is only necessary to write down the sum 779×91 in order to appreciate the difference; in Roman numerals we have to write DCCLXXIX $\times$ XCI. The Arabic system of numerals introduced the number 0 together with a systematic and unimpeachable decimal structure, thus achieving a definite advantage for practical counting, though its superiority goes further than that of course. According to Leibniz, the natural numbers are defined by the following chain of definition: $2 = 1 + 1$, $3 = 2 + 1$, etc. Here all numbers which are expressed by Arabic numerals (after the series of ten numbers has been learned) immediately show the position of the designated number in the chain of definition. Thus, the representation of a number in Arabic numerals immediately gives its definition, and this, according to Leibniz, is its real definition. From this is follows that a longer number is always a larger number, so that a relation between numerals is a direct expression of the relation between the numbers which they express.

We now come to the question of whether the decimal system or some other system based upon some other unit is the more convenient. The system which immediately suggests itself is the dyadic system, in that it makes use of only two signs, 0 and 1. The two systems of numbers can be easily combined: $1 = 1$, $2 = 10$, $3 = 11$, $4 = 100$, $5 = 101$, etc. Leibniz was extremely interested in the dyadic (binary) system (GM VII, 223 ff.). It has become very important in the construction of modern computers, although Leibniz probably over-estimated its theoretical importance.

The problems of the *characteristica universalis* also arise in the differential and integral calculus and form, as we have seen in § 9, a part of the difference between Leibniz and Newton. Newton terms the first differential quotient $x^{\cdot}$, the second, $x^{\cdot\cdot}$, the third, $x^{\cdot\cdot\cdot}$, whilst Leibniz chooses for these three quotients the terms:

$$\frac{dx}{dy} \qquad \frac{d^2x}{dy^2} \qquad \frac{d^3x}{dy^3}$$

Now, it is true that here too the terms are quite arbitrary, with the essential difference lying in the fact that in Leibniz's system the quantity with respect to which the differentiation is carried out is expressed, whereas this is not the case in Newton's system. From this it follows that Newton's system is only reasonable where the differentiation is always carried out in respect of the same variables and for Newton this is what happens. He is primarily concerned with physical dimensions, especially speed and acceleration, and thus only needs the first or second differential quotients in respect of time. The Newtonian system is completely satisfactory for this purpose and is still used today within these limits. If we are, however, to consider general problems from a purely analytic standpoint, it is clear that differential quotients based upon all sorts of variables can arise and in these cases the Leibnizian system is without doubt the more effective.

The *ars characteristica* then proceeds from this question of the greater or lesser suitability of particular signs to the second and more general question of the overall necessity for and significance of signs. Leibniz says in this general sense that the *ars* belongs to metaphysics:

'The abstract doctrine of signs, which is the universal characteristic and belongs to metaphysics' (GM VII, 24).

We see here a close link with Hobbes, who regarded thinking as a form of calculation. In any case, we can say that in mathematics and physics, the sciences in which Leibniz was interested, signs are a necessity. Leibniz then seems to have gone on to argue that signs were necessary for all kinds of thought. He probably agreed with Huygens that 'the human mind has need of signs for thinking' (GM II, 117).

Signs are the subject of Leibniz's treatise: *Dialogus de connexione inter res et verba, et veritatis realitate*. This dialogue did not appear until 1756 when it was published by Raspe, nevertheless I believe that it may be regarded as a finished work. In it Leibniz points out the necessity of expressing thought by words or symbols:

B. 'What then? Thoughts are possible without words.'

A. 'But not without other signs. I wonder whether you could make any mathematical calculations without numerals.'

B. 'You disturb me greatly, for I did not think that signs or symbols were so necessary for thought.'

A. 'Then arithmetical truths suppose certain signs or symbols?'
B. 'Agreed' (GP VII, 191).

Although the necessity for signs is here only shown for arithmetic they are required for every form of thought, as we see from Huygens's letter. The idea that every form of thought requires signs and that these differ as regards suitability leads to the task of investigating the connection between thoughts and signs (*connexio inter res et verba*) which is the general task of the *ars characteristica*. Leibniz gave a great deal of thought to this problem, though most of his writings on it were not published. They have been made available in part by nineteenth-century editors and Couturat has published more of them. If the collected works publish the material in full it will extend far beyond that which is at present available, though it is doubtful whether this greater volume will increase our knowledge of the essentials.

The significance of the problem for the differential and integral calculus is, I feel, clear. The means by which Leibniz made his discoveries in this field depend largely upon the fact that he reflected on the need for signs in the new *scientia infiniti* and, conversely, the successes of the *ars characteristica* in the new discipline caused Leibniz to set such great store by it.

Leibniz's ideas on the significance of signs are of interest in the interpretation of Kantian philosophy and for many more modern purposes. The idea leads to a constructivist point of view, that is to say, it leads to a point of view which recognises the significance of construction and of intuition in mathematical thought. At first glance, exactly the reverse seems to be the case. The introduction of signs seems to imply a purely analytic standpoint and hence the rejection of geometric intuition. This lies behind Huygens's statement:

'And hence by the most simple calculation, without regard to any figure, is derived the famous property of tangents to cycloids, which we express thus . . .' (GM II, 118).

The new infinitesimal calculus makes it possible to determine the properties of curves, in the case of cycloids, without the need for a pictorial representation of them. In this sense analytic calculus rejects geometric intuition; on the other hand using the analytic calculus is itself operating with signs, constructing signs and groups of signs, transposing signs, in general manipulating signs. For the very reason that analytic calculus is concerned with signs it becomes once more related to intuition, a very reduced intuition it is true, an intuition of signs. Kant carries this idea through to its logical conclusion when he forms the concept of symbolical construction in arithmetic, where he regards construction and therefore intuition as necessities of arithmetic. Here is a possible connection between Leibniz and Kant which escaped me in my dissertation. I now find it necessary to point out that Kant probably paid the utmost attention to Raspe's edition of Leibniz and he would have found ample support for his theories in the *Dialogus de connexione inter res et verba*. In this case, Kant's doctrine of the synthetic character of arithmetic may well be based upon Leibniz's notion of the *ars characteristica*; perhaps a not unfruitful line of investigation.[26]

§ 14. SCIENTIA GENERALIS

The new sciences which we are attempting to expound in this chapter vary considerably as to the degree in which they have been realised. Differential and integral calculus are among the basic constituents of our mathematical and scientific thought and Leibniz, simultaneously with Newton, developed them to an advanced state. In dynamics Leibniz remains very much a traditionalist and here cannot be compared with Newton. The *analysis situs* is a well-founded doctrine but this had to wait until the nineteenth century for its realisation, and the same is true of the *scientia de relationibus* which also had to wait for the nineteenth and the twentieth centuries for its realisation. Of the *ars characteristica* it may be said that it has a very sound basis but that up to now only its first beginnings have been realised. On the other hand, I would say of the *scientia generalis*, disagreeing with Couturat and Kabitz, that it is a plan which is not capable of realisation, nothing more than a Utopia.

We find the term *scientia generalis* in a number of places. Erdmann published two manuscripts to which Leibniz gave this title. Manuscript XII is called: *Initia scientiae generalis de nova ratione instaurationis et augmentationis scientiarum, ita ut exiguo tempore et negotio, si modo velint homines, magna praestari possunt ad felicitatis humane incrementum*; the second, Number XIV in Erdmann's edition, is called by Leibniz: *Synopsis libri, cui titulus erit: Scientia nova generalis pro instauratione et augmentis scientiarum ad publicam felicitatem* (GP VII, 49).

Other manuscripts have for the most part only been published fragmentarily. There are numerous manuscripts in the *Opera Philosophica* edited by Erdmann and in the philosophical and mathematical writings edited by Gerhardt. At the turn of the century, Couturat started to pay special attention to the *scientia generalis* which then became the fulcrum of his exposition of Leibniz's work and of his edition. Mahnke has shown in § 2 just how great is the significance of the *scientia generalis* for Couturat's interpretation of Leibniz.

I have found the best summary of the *scientia generalis* in a letter to the Duke John Frederick written in October 1671. Leibniz wrote this letter because he wished to apply for the post of librarian in Wolfenbüttel, the position which was to, and which did, provide him with the support necessary to allow him to continue his work. He had, therefore, to give a résumé both of the work which he had done up to that time and of the work which he hoped to do in the future. From this point of view, the *scientia generalis* is for him the most important thing and so he writes:

'In philosophy I have discovered a method of achieving in all sciences, by means of the *ars combinatoria*, what Descartes and others have achieved in arithmetic and geometry by algebra and analysis. This *ars* was first developed by Lull and P. Kircher but they were far from recognising all its potentialities. By its means all notions in the world can be reduced to a few simple terms which serve as an alphabet and by using combinations of this alphabet a means will be found to discover systematically all things together with their theorems and whatever can be found out about them. This invention, in so far as God willing it may be put to work, is considered by me to be the mother of all inventions and to be the most important of all, even though it may not be recognised as such at the moment. I have, by its means, discovered everything that is now to be related and I hope to discover even more' (GP I, 57).

Even though Leibniz never brought this plan for a *scientia generalis* to fruition, his objects are made clear in this letter.

The plan originally consisted of two parts, the *initia* and the *specimina*. Leibniz uses the phrase *initia scientiae generalis* in the title which we quoted above; he talks in several other places of the *specimina* which are concerned with separate disciplines to be constructed in accordance with the total plan. Among them would be included those sciences which we have already mentioned, the *scientia infiniti*, the *scientia dynamica* and the *scientia de relationibus in universum*. In one sense, then, it could be maintained that only the first part of the *initia scientiae generalis* constitutes the science for which Leibniz was seeking. It would then fall into two further parts:

'The *Scientia generalis* contains two parts of which the first pertains to the renovation of sciences and would judge those that have already been discovered; the second is concerned with the expansion of science and with the invention of those sciences which do not yet exist' (E 85*a*).

This second part of the *initia scientiae generalis* was shortly afterwards termed the *scientia inveniendo* by Leibniz, who was most probably influenced by the possibilities of infinitesimal calculus in developing this term *ars inveniendi*. This form of calculus permits results, which up to this time had been sought for and achieved one by one, to be achieved systematically by calculation. Problems of this type are, for example, tangents or the maxima and minima of curves. It is from this that Leibniz, no doubt, gained the idea of an *ars inveniendi*, which might offer a systematic form of calculation for any problem whatever.

The first part of the *initia*, which Leibniz elsewhere calls the *elementa veritatis aeterna*[27] and here *notae indisputabiles*, is by far the most important. We must assume that the term *nota indisputabilis* is very carefully chosen. Ideally this doctrine of the elements of truth should embrace the absolute, fundamental concepts and trace the proof of all true propositions back to these fundamentals. As, however, these absolute, fundamental concepts are as yet unknown to us we are forced to accept fundamental concepts which can be accepted as such for the particular problem in hand. Such concepts may be susceptible of further analysis, but for the present problem they can be considered as being no longer subject to discussion, as *indisputabiles*. These fundamental concepts—either the absolute fundamental concepts or those which are relatively fundamental in respect of a certain problem—can then be represented by a suitable system of signs and can be subjected to the calculus:

'So that all argument proceeds in legitimate form after the fashion of the calculus of numbers; if any mistake crept in, its detection would be no more difficult and its revelation no harder than customary errors of the calculus' (E 85a).

This is not always possible and we are therefore driven to considerations of probability, but where this process can be carried out the argument is at an end. There is just as little need for argument upon this point as there is over the sum or product of two numbers. We need only say, 'Let us calculate.' This is the only objective solution to any problem and would follow in the footsteps of the creator: 'When God thinks and calculates, the world is created.' There is no doubt that the courage and consistency of the *scientia generalis* is attractive and we are constantly aware in Couturat's work how great has been its influence upon him. Kabitz, too, regards the *scientia generalis* as a discovery of genius.[28] It is not, we feel, a coincidence that Leibniz kept this discovery among his papers. The systematic opposition to his plan will be discussed later, but we should like to feel that Huygens was right in his scepticism when he wrote to Leibniz on 22 January 1679: 'I tell you quite simply that I think these are but pleasant dreams and I should need further proof to believe that there is any reality in what you suggest' (GM II, 28).

CHAPTER V

THE THEORY OF SCIENCE

§ 15. FINITE AND INFINITE SYSTEMS

THE fundamental feature of the pure sciences is the coherence of their propositions, which means that certain propositions can be proved by others. It is the task of the theory of science to consider this coherence as such. Leibniz himself did not regard the theory of science as a separate discipline, but his works offer a wealth of observations which belong under this heading.

Leibniz recognized that the propositions of a particular science are interdependent.

'Are we supposed to believe that truths exist in our understanding independently of one another, just as the edicts of the praetor were listed on his tablet or his notice board?' (GP V, 81).

Leibniz also realized that it was the specific achievement of the Greek mathematicians to have been the first to observe this coherence.

'It must be admitted that the Greeks argued with all possible exactitude in mathematics and left us the models of the art of proof, for even if the Babylonians and the Egyptians had something more than a purely empirical geometry, nothing of it has been preserved' (GP V, 352).

On the basis of his combinatorial theory of concepts, Leibniz sees two classes of systems: compound concepts may contain an infinite number of component concepts or a finite number; systems which only contain concepts with a finite number of component concepts we shall call finite systems, all others infinite systems. Infinite systems would then embrace concepts with an infinite number of component concepts, in so far as these exist. The problem is made more difficult in Leibniz's work by the fact that there are no precise definitions of finite concepts and that he changes his point of view with regard to infinite concepts.

The problem of concepts which consist of a finite number of component concepts depends upon two presuppositions: that there are concepts which cannot be further reduced, and that there are compound concepts which can be reduced in a finite number of steps to indissoluble fundamental concepts. There are passages where Leibniz discusses these presuppositions, for example the letter to Vagetius of 2 December 1679 (GP VII, 292), and a passage published by Couturat:

'We ask therefore whether it is possible for the resolution of noncomplex terms to be carried on to infinity, so that we never arrive at the concepts in themselves. Certainly if we have no notions within us conceived in themselves which we can reach distinctly, or only one, the notion of being, it follows that no proposition can have a completely rational demonstration' (Inédits, p. 373).

On the other hand, we have Aristotle's view that a *regressus in infinitum* is not possible in a chain of proof (81 b, 10 ff.). In the *De arte combinatoria* Leibniz, referring to Aristotle, assumes the existence of fundamental concepts which can be arrived at after a finite number of steps (GP IV, 65). In the *Meditationes*, written in 1684, Leibniz maintains the same position; though admitting that we may find it hard to achieve:

'when analysis has been taken to its conclusion . . . but I do not know whether men are capable of giving a perfect example of this' (GP IV, 423).

If we bear this difficulty in mind, and if I understand the position correctly, Leibniz's argument is that concepts from the realm of rational truths (the *vérités de raison*), that is the concepts of logic and mathematics, as well as many metaphysical concepts, are concepts of a finite degree of composition and these concepts contain only a finite number of component concepts. The example of the natural numbers shows that this does not conflict with the infinite nature of these systems. Every natural number is composed of a finite number of prime numbers but there is, at the same time, an infinite number of natural numbers. There would be no difficulty here. On the other hand, it is difficult to understand how Leibniz, who made some of the most important discoveries in the field of infinite series, could have applied a finite theory of concepts to them.

In contrast to concepts from the realm of the rational sciences, the concepts of factual science are of an infinite degree of composition and here we do, in fact, find a change of theoretical attitude. At first, Leibniz excluded factual concepts from the sphere of his combinatorial theory of concepts and thereby from the analytic theory of judgement. Later he included them but regarded them as concepts of infinite composition thus giving them a special position.

The early position is clearly expressed in the *De arte combinatoria*:

'Then it must be remembered that the whole of this complex art is directed towards theorems or propositions of eternal truth which exist not by the will of God but through their own nature. Indeed all singular propositions, such as historical ones (Augustus was a Roman emperor) or observations, that is universal propositions, the truth of which is based upon existence and not essence, are truths as if by accident, that is by the will of God. For example, "all adult men in Europe have knowledge of God". Such propositions are given not by demonstration but by induction' (GP IV, 69).

Later, however, perhaps as the *Monadology* began to take shape, Leibniz changes his point of view: there are now concepts, in the sense of the combinatorial theory of concepts, of all empirical objects. There is a concept of Augustus and in this concept is contained the fact that Augustus was a Roman emperor. This particular Augustus had to become a Roman emperor because it is a part of his concept: an Augustus who was not a Roman emperor would have been different in a thousand other ways. Hence, these concepts, for example the concept of Augustus, contain an infinite number of partial concepts. They are no longer resolvable in our human understanding. On the other hand, they are capable of being intuited and comprehended by God's infinite understanding and so God also sees the necessity of Augustus's being a Roman emperor.

This changed attitude is expressed in the manuscript which Erdmann called: *De scientia universali seu calculo philosophico* in which Leibniz says:

'The distinction between necessary and contingent truths is the same as that between commensurable and incommensurable numbers, for as with incommensurable numbers the resolution may be found in a common measure, so in necessary truths the proof or reduction to identical truths takes place. Just as in imperfect reasons the resolution proceeds to infinity and indeed approaches in a sense to a common measure or acquires a certain, though unfinished, series, so by the same process contingent truths are equally in need of infinite analysis which God alone is capable of comprehending. Hence they are known by Him alone *a priori* and with certainty' (GP VII, 200).

This manuscript cannot be an early one as the *Meditationes* of 1684 are quoted in it.

Russell expounds Leibniz's point of view by saying that only the propositions of the *a priori* sciences are analytic propositions, the propositions of factual science being synthetic (p. 16); but as far as I can see this only applies to Leibniz's early work. In the *Monadology* the factual sciences are also subject to the analytic theory of judgement, though with restrictions which stem from the infinite character of these concepts for our finite human understanding.

§ 16. AXIOMATISABLE SYSTEMS

We shall confine our remarks on Leibniz's theory of systems to rational systems, that is, in the first place, to mathematics. Euclid's *Elements* have been for two thousand years the starting point of all investigations into the nature of axioms. The *Elements* begin with definitions, axioms and postulates and this structure has naturally afforded mathematicians, logicians and philosophers the liveliest interest.

It was soon recognised that the definitions were not used in the development of the *Elements* and this clearly raises a delicate question of which Leibniz is well aware. In his correspondence with Giordano on the fundamentals of geometry Leibniz points out that although Giordano himself gives a definition of a straight line, he does not use it in his geometry. The only conclusion to be drawn from this is that the propositions concerning the straight line could, in fact, apply to any line whatever (GM I, 196). The same could be said of Euclid. It has never been established that there is any essential difference between postulates and axioms. Leibniz scarcely observed this distinction, and we shall also ignore it.

There are two possible points of view with regard to axioms. Either they are truly axioms, that is undemonstrable propositions; or they are not genuine axioms, but demonstrable propositions which have not so far been proved. They remain axioms only until a proof has been found. If they are truly axioms, then we can assume that they are very closely connected with the essential laws of space, since all other laws of space follow from them. In this case we must assume a special kind of knowledge for the comprehension of their truth, different from our knowledge of the truth of derived propositions. Aristotle must have understood the axioms of geometry in approximately this sense and in our own day Husserl regarded them in this way.

The truly axiomatic nature of axioms is denied if all so-called axioms are regarded as demonstrable propositions. This was Leibniz's own view. He was perpetually seeking to prove the axioms and was intensely interested in all the earlier attempts to prove them.

'This is more or less the case with those propositions which are generally regarded as axioms, but which, like the theorems could be proved and are worth proving; nevertheless they are permitted to function as axioms as though they were original truths. Such indulgence does more harm than one thinks; yet we are not in position to renounce it' (GP V, 156).

Leibniz draws attention to the attempts at proving the axioms and mentions particularly Apollonius, Proclus and Roberval (GP V, 387). These two references to the *Nouveaux Essais* may suffice to represent the numerous passages in which he demands a proof of the axioms.

There now arises the question of how to prove the axioms. In the *Nouveaux Essais* Leibniz indicates a possible method of proof.

'I have often mentioned, both in private and in public, that it would be important to prove all the secondary axioms, of which we normally make use, by reducing them to the original, that is the immediate and undemonstrable axioms, which I have latterly and also elsewhere termed identical' (GP V, 388).

This is in fact for Leibniz the only possible and hence the necessary method of proof and for this reason Leibniz can say in the *Initia rerum mathematicarum metaphysica*, which he did not himself publish:

'Hence we see the proofs finally resolved into two undemonstrables: definitions or ideas, and original or identical propositions, of the type "B is B", "a thing is equal to itself" and an infinite number of other propositions of this sort' (GM VII, 20).

We saw in § 6 that Leibniz understood by identical propositions either absolutely identical propositions of the form B is B or the virtually identical propositions of the form AB is B. Absolutely identical propositions are clear in themselves, virtually identical propositions are simply expanded definitions. Definitions are thus seen to be the final basis of all proofs and Leibniz can write to Conring on 19 March 1678: 'proof is a chain of definitions' (GP I. 194).

It may be worthwhile giving some concrete examples of Leibniz's train of thought. We have seen that for Leibniz the problem of the derivability of syllogisms consists of the derivability of the *modus barbara*. Leibniz's theories of the concept and of judgement permit him to resolve the *modus barbara* in the following way:

$$ABC \text{ is } BC$$
$$BC \text{ is } C$$
$$\therefore ABC \text{ is } C$$

The *modus barbara* consists, therefore, if this solution is correct, of a chain of definitions and identical propositions.

As a second example we take the proposition: if two quantities are equal to a third, they are equal to each other, a proposition which appears as an axiom in Euclid. It can be regarded either as belonging to the general theory of mathematics or of quantities, or, because of the relative character of equality to the general theory of relations. There is a proof of this in the essay: *Non inelegans specimen demonstrandi abstractis*. Although this paper remained in manuscript, it is so far developed that it could for all practical purposes be regarded as ready for publication (GP VII, 228 ff.).

Leibniz begins with the following definition of equality:

'Definition I: Those things are the same of which one could be substituted for the other while maintaining the truth. If they are A and B and A enters some other true proposition and then in one place by substituting B for this same A, a new proposition is made, which is equally true, and this always happens in any such proposition, A and B are said to be the same: and conversely if A and B are the same, substitution may proceed as I have said' (GP VII, 228).

Further definitions, explanations of symbols, two axioms and two postulates follow, but these are not used in our proof. Leibniz then presents the proposition and the proof in the following form:

'Theorem I: two things which are equal to a third are equal to each other. If $A = B$ and $B = C$, A will $= C$. For if in the proposition $A = B$ (true from the hypothesis) C is substituted in the place of B (which we may do because of Definition I since $B = C$ ex. hyp.) then $A = C$ QED' (GP VII, 230).

This proof is particularly characteristic both on account of its brevity and its lucidity. It was required to prove a fundamental principle of equality which up till then had been regarded as an axiom. The proof succeeds by means of finding a definition of the concept of equality from which the proof can then be adduced with the utmost brevity, a plausible method in the case of so fundamental a proposition. It can be seen that the whole burden of the problem is shifted to the definition upon which everything now depends. However, we must bear in mind that the substitution used here for the definition of equality differs from the one normally used in modern logic. First, Leibniz's substitution may only be used in true propositions, that is it cannot be used, like the modern substitution, in any proposition. Nor is it necessary. in the formulation in which the substitution is to be effected, to replace the variable for which the substitution is being made in every position in which it occurs. Leibniz says rather that it is only necessary to substitute in one place (*in aliquo loco*). Furthermore, it is significant that the definition of equality which is used here is hard to reconcile with Leibniz's general theory of definition, for this definition is not of the form *homo = animal rationale*, and does not consist of reducing the concept of equality to its partial concepts. Finally, however, a new problem is raised (one which we shall discuss in the next section), by the question as to whether the chosen definition is possible at all, that is, whether it is free from contradiction. Although such a justification of the definition is needed, there is no trace of it, at least in the *Specimen*. This lucid example shows that the working out of Leibniz's idea of proof is burdened with many difficulties.

It is natural that Leibniz was specially concerned about the axioms of geometry. Among his papers there is an essay on this subject (GM V, 183), but it is merely another exposition of the same basic ideas and does not add anything essentially new.

It is no easy task to evaluate this fundamental idea of the theory of proof: *demonstratio est catena definitionum*, since it could only be judged if it was fully worked out. Technically, it amounts to this: geometry does not begin with axioms but with definitions. David Hilbert followed the diametrically opposite course and replaced definitions by axioms, even going so far as to reject nominal definitions.[29] For example, he offers no nominal definition of a straight line, but regards the axioms which deal with the straight line in their totality as an implicit definition. In the light of later developments, therefore, we are bound to have considerable reservations about Leibniz's theory of proof. We shall endeavour to show in the next section that, even accepting Leibniz's own presuppositions, there are serious objections to the underlying idea of the theory.

Leibniz's concept of geometrical proof can be presented in another way which allows it to be tested by modern methods. As we saw in the correspondence with Clarke, Leibniz considered that mathematics and especially geometry sprang solely from the principle of contradiction:

'The great foundation of mathematics is the principle of contradiction or of identity, that is that a statement cannot be false and true at the same time, and that thus A is A and can never be non-A and this one principle is enough to prove the whole of arithmetic and the whole of geometry, that is, all mathematical principles' (2nd letter).

The rejection of true axioms and the use of definition and identical propositions as the only pre-suppositions in geometry are the consequences of this approach.

Leibniz gives another instructive example in the *Theodicy*:

'It is quite different in the case of the dimensions of matter. The three-fold number is determined here not by the reason of the best but by geometrical necessity: and this for the reason that the geometers can demonstrate that only three straight lines can intersect at right angles' (§ 351).

If three-dimensional Euclidian geometry can spring from the principle of contradiction alone, this means that every other type of geometry contains a contradiction within itself. Hence it follows that the so-called axioms of geometry can be demonstrated from the principle of contradiction alone and thus the truly axiomatic character of geometry is lost. The twenty-three-year-old Kant noticed that Leibniz gives no proof of this statement. At this time Kant regarded other geometries as being free from contradiction, at least with regard to dimensionality. In this way he recognised their possibility and so furthered their realisation. There is no reason to suppose that Kant changed his mind about this lack of contradiction at a later date, indeed, he seems to have found confirmation for his opinion in Lambert's work on non-Euclidian geometry. His opinion could be summed up as follows: under the sole criterion of freedom from contradiction, other geometries besides three-dimensional Euclidian geometry are possible. However, Kant required a further condition of existence, namely constructability in intuition. Under this double condition of existence, freedom from contradiction and constructability in intuition, Kant took the view in the *Critique of Pure Reason* that Euclidian geometry is the only possible one.

The argument may today be regarded as settled. Geometries other than three-dimensional Euclidian geometry are free from contradiction. There are two decisive considerations. First, analytical geometry can express other geometries besides three-dimensional Euclidian geometry. Further, Euclidian models of non-Euclidian geometry have been discovered, first by Poincaré, so that non-Euclidian geometries can be expressed in Euclidian space. Both of these methods demonstrate the freedom from contradiction of non-Euclidian geometry. If there were a contradiction contained in them it would show up in analysis and by way of the Euclidian models even in Euclidian geometry itself. Thus it is certain that there is no difference between Euclidian geometry and the established non-Euclidian geometries in respect of freedom from contradiction, which certainly invalidates Leibniz's approach to the theory of proof in geometry. It is not true that Euclidian geometry can be derived from the principle of contradiction alone, and it is not true that the so-called axioms of geometry can be proved by the principle of contradiction. Kant was right: geometry rests on genuine axioms.

§ 17. FREEDOM FROM CONTRADICTION

Scientific systems are further typified by their freedom from contradiction. If, for example, a contradiction is admitted into a mathematical system, then by using this contradiction it is possible to prove any desired contradiction and thereby every possible proposition. Leibniz knew this when he said in the *Meditationes* (1684):

'For we are unable to use definitions in order to reach a conclusion until we know that they are real and do not involve any contradiction. The reason for this is that from ideas involving contradictions we can reach opposite conclusions at the same time, which is absurd' (GP IV, 424).

This would be both absurd and at the same time the end of all science. However, the enormous range that Leibniz accords to the principle of contradiction makes the problem of freedom from contradiction specially important for him. We have seen that the *principium contradictionis* is the necessary and sufficient condition of existence for the *a priori* sciences, that it is the necessary condition for all the empirical sciences, and that the unconditional validity of the principle has its basis in divine thought, which is the source of all rational and all factual truths.

Leibniz saw that there was a whole series of concepts which appear at first sight completely above suspicion, but which upon closer examination prove to contain contradictions. In the *Meditationes de cognitione, veritate et ideis* he discusses the concept of the greatest velocity. This apparently innocent concept can easily be shown, by means of an experiment in thought, to contain a contradiction. It is possible to imagine a wheel which revolves at such a speed that the points upon its periphery move with the hypothetically greatest velocity. It is then possible to embark on the experiment and extend a spoke of the wheel; every point upon the extended spoke will then move at a greater speed than any point on the periphery. The argument is conclusive under the principles of classical physics which were valid for Leibniz.

A further example is the concept of the greatest number (*numerus numerorum* or *numerus maximus*). If numbers are counted consecutively, then there are exactly ten numbers up to ten, exactly a hundred up to a hundred. The last number is therefore the greatest number, *numerus maximus* and at the same time counts the number of numbers, *numerus numerorum*. From here one may proceed to ask how many numbers there are in all, meaning the natural series of numbers. To attempt to answer this would immediately involve one in difficulties. Every natural number is either odd or even, but is the *numerus maximus* or *numerus numerorum* odd or even? Presumably neither, but how can there be a natural number which does not have this fundamental characteristic of all natural numbers? Leibniz argues in a manner which is very close to the modern view. Against the concept of the greatest number must be set the limitless ability of numbers to be increased, an increase which can be achieved by both multiplication and addition and it must therefore be shown that every natural number is capable of being multiplied or added to. Leibniz chooses the latter way. For every natural number there exists a number which is twice as great, the number 2n. 2n is always greater than n, zero being disregarded. Thus if N were the greatest number there would nevertheless be a number 2N, which is however, by definition, greater than N, and so the concept contains a contradiction (GM III, 535). Leibniz is here using arguments known to antiquity, which have been fully vindicated in recent times.

Freedom from contradiction plays an important part in Leibniz's discussion of the Cartesian ontological proof of God in his *Meditationes*. The ontological proof rests on a concept similar to those which we have been discussing. God is defined as *omnitudo realitatis*; existence must be included in this *omnitudo realitatis*, since existence itself is a reality; therefore God as the *omnitudo realitatis* must also have existence (GP IV, 424).

Leibniz objects that this proof would be invalid if the underlying concept of God contained a contradiction. For then, Leibniz must have argued, it would be possible to prove both the existence and the non-existence of God from the contradictory concept of the *omnitudo realitatis*. This means that the ontological proof of God must remain incomplete until the underlying concept of God as *omnitudo realitatis* is proved. Leibniz must have been convinced that it would not be easy to close this gap. The argument over the ontological proof of God is a very important one for Leibniz, who hastens to point out that Thomas Aquinas had doubts about the proof. Kant, too, joined in the criticism of the ontological proof of God, though for different reasons.

On the basis of these examples all concepts which contain the concepts of a totality or of maximum and minimum must be regarded as suspicious. This is a harsh statement for the seventeenth century, at least as far as the concepts of maximum and minimum are concerned, in view of the part these concepts played in the great discoveries of the century, integral and differential calculus. Their significance is so great that Leibniz himself often calls the new method, the *methodus de maximis et minimis*. On the other hand, we must admire the genius of the great thinker who saw that these concepts of totalities were the source of the difficulties and our admiration is only heightened when we remember the trouble Kant and modern thinkers have had in clarifying them sufficiently to see the concept of a totality as the source of fundamental antimonies.

In order to proceed with the systematic treatment of the

question of freedom from contradiction it will be necessary to see where contradictions can and do arise. On the basis of Leibnizian philosophy contradictions cannot arise from logical deduction or from the process of proof. A logical process or a process of proof which calls forth contradictions is not a legitimate one for it means that a mistake must have been made, which cannot escape careful investigation. There remain only among Leibniz's presuppositions definitions and identical propositions and here again absolutely identical propositions of the form B is B cannot be the source of contradiction. A virtually identical proposition could contain a contradiction, but only inasmuch as it derives the predicate B from the compound subject AB. A contradiction could only exist between component concepts of the subject. Thus concepts and the definitions which correspond to them are the only possible sources of contradictions. In order to study this question Leibniz returns in the *Meditationes* to the old thesis that definitions are arbitrary, stating that it is possible to define anything but that one is then bound by the condition that definitions which are of themselves arbitrary should not contain a contradiction ('*nullam involvere contradictionem*'). Now we have seen that for Leibniz freedom from contradiction is the necessary and sufficient condition for possibility and thus for the possibility of definitions and concepts. At this point Leibniz changes the meaning of the term nominal definition, which traditionally indicates the meaning of a term. The nominal definition of a decahedron determines it as a regular body which is bounded by ten congruent surfaces. Traditional nominal definition leaves the question as to the possibility of such a body open, but since the decahedron contains a contradiction within itself, there is for Leibniz, no idea, no definition, not even a nominal definition of a decahedron, which remains for him an empty word.

'For it is not in our power in either science to make combinations at will, otherwise we should have the right to talk of a regular decahedron' (GP V, 301).

Thus no one is justified in talking of a decahedron, which is a mere sound with neither sense nor meaning. Leibniz in this way makes a new distinction between nominal and real definition. A nominal definition is a definition which permits us to identify a non-contradictory and therefore possible ideal or real object; from a real definition it is possible to recognise the possibility of the object which means, in the case of an ideal object, the ability to discern its freedom from contradiction.

'And so we also have a distinction between nominal definitions which contain signs to distinguish one thing from another and real definitions from which we determine that the thing is possible' (GP IV, 424).

This leads us on to the idea that a judgement is contained in every definition, the judgement, that is to say, that the object defined is free from contradiction, and is a possible object. This is particularly evident in the case of real definitions.

'As far as the proposition "three is two plus one" is concerned which you put forward as an example of intuitive knowledge, I would remark that this is merely the definition of the expression three, for the most simple definitions of numbers are formed thus: two is one plus one, three is two plus one, four is three plus one, etc. Nevertheless, as I have remarked, a judgement is concealed here, namely that these ideas are possible; and this is recognised intuitively here' (GP V, 347).

There is no doubt that the problem of finding reasons for possible contradictions and of evolving a method of proving freedom from contradiction is a thorny one and Leibniz often complains about it:

'There are two gaps, which are more difficult to fill, the one is that doubt exists as to whether certain ideas are consistent with each other, as long as experience shews us that they are not linked to the same object' (GP V, 318).

Leibniz's assumptions only allow contradictions to occur in definitions, but concepts correspond to definitions and concepts are assumed to be either simple or compound. The first possible source of contradictions could be fundamental concepts which are contradictory in themselves; such do not exist for Leibniz. The second possibility would be that certain fundamental concepts contradict each other. If, for example, the fundamental concepts L and M contradicted each other a contradiction would arise if in a compound concept the two fundamental concepts L and M appeared as partial concepts. Leibniz made no final and definitive statement about this, nevertheless I think it may be assumed that he did not accept the possibility of contradictions between simple fundamental concepts. In the *Meditationes*, for example, he often equates fundamental concepts with the old concept of the *attributa Dei* which cannot contain a contradiction. But even if we leave theological considerations aside, there seems no possibility of a contradiction between simple fundamental concepts. A contradiction presupposes that a set of circumstances can simultaneously be affirmed and negated and a contradiction cannot occur without the composition implied in the concept of negation. If simple fundamental concepts were capable of contradicting each other, then we should have no possibility, owing to the simplicity of these concepts, of recognising and avoiding these contradictions and the whole situation would be hopeless. It can therefore be said that, in the opinion of Leibniz, fundamental concepts cannot contradict each other.

The problem is, then, reduced to the one possibility: a contradiction arises when in a compound concept a partial concept is present together with its negation. This form of contradiction is specifically mentioned by Leibniz. 'A false term is one which contains opposites, A and non-A.' This is at least one way in which contradictions may occur and it is impossible to envisage, within the framework of Leibniz's thought, any other way in which contradictions could arise. For example, a contradiction would be implied if man were designated an *irrational animal*. This *homo irrationalis* would be irrational, and if one accepts the definition of man as *animal rationale*, this represents for Leibniz a contradiction both in form and content.

If then, the reason for contradictions lies in the presence of a partial concept and its negation in the same compound concept, a method can be evolved for recognising and avoiding such contradictions. This is the method of analysis by which a compound concept is reduced to its component parts thus showing that such a contradiction is not present. This, however, pre-supposes adequate knowledge and a completed analysis.

'And indeed whenever there is adequate knowledge, there is also *a priori* knowledge of possibility: if the analysis has been brought to a conclusion and no contradiction has become apparent, the notion is possible' (GP IV, 425).

It is difficult to achieve such a complete analysis and so Leibniz continues sadly:

'But whether it is ever possible for man to achieve a perfect analysis of notions or whether he can direct his thought back to first possibilities or to ideas which are not capable of further resolution, I would not now dare to say.'

However, as it is necessary to prove freedom from contradiction, Leibniz has to seek a different way and he finds it in the *a posteriori* method. If we can determine from experience that a certain object exists, then the concept which designates it is possible and so free from contradiction. *Definitiones causales*, which tell us how an object can be constructed, now become very valuable.

This leads to a remarkable consequence in mathematics. The being of the objects of geometry and arithmetic is primarily determined as a pure being in itself (*Ansichsein*, to use the modern term). However, the above arguments introduce strong empirical and constructive considerations into mathematics, since only in this manner can freedom from contradiction be proved. In arithmetic Leibniz recognised the need for a recursive definition for natural numbers: (2 = 1 plus 1, 3 = 2 plus 1, 4 = 3 plus 1, etc.); we have now seen that these definitions must be shown to be free from contradiction, a point upon which Leibniz is quite clear.

'We are not actually stating a truth when we say that one and one are two, we are rather defining two. Nevertheless, it is true and evident, that it is the definition of a possible object' (GP V, 390).

What does Leibniz mean when he defines the insight into possibility, that is into the freedom from contradiction of two, as evident? He surely can only be referring to inner experience. We can often observe in our inner experience that we have two wishes or two thoughts and are thus aware of the existence of two objects from which the existence of two itself would be intuitively and evidently determined. The same would then be true of three, four and whole series of consecutive numbers, and Leibniz apparently also regards it as evident that the process continues without contradiction beyond the smaller and immediately evident numbers.

The same consideration leads to a strongly constructive point of view in geometry, where the real definition of a geometric figure should give its construction and at the same time its possibility. This is, for example, true of the Euclidian definition of a circle: 'but the idea of a circle proposed by Euclid, which would be a figure described by motion of a line in a plane about one fixed end, is a real definition, for it is clear that such a figure is possible. Hence it is useful to have definitions involving the generation of a thing, or at least if that is lacking, the constitution, i.e. the way in which it appears producible or at least possible' (GP VII, 294).

Every property which is true of an object and of it alone can be used as a definition, but such a property does not necessarily contain the proof of possibility. Thus a circle could be defined as a figure whose peripheral angles are all equal. This is a property of a circle and only of a circle, but according to Leibniz, at least, this definition does not allow us to prove that such a figure is possible (GP I, 385).[30]

We find considerations of this sort repeatedly in Leibniz's writings.

'Henceforth the most perfect real definitions are those which agree with all hypotheses or modes of production and from which the possibility of the thing is immediately obvious. Naturally, there is no presupposed experiment, nor any pre-supposed proof of the possibility of another thing. This occurs when the thing is resolved into pure notions understood through themselves: such knowledge I generally call adequate or intuitive; thus if anything was repugnant, it would at once appear so, since there would be no room for further reductions' (GP VII, 295).

If we try to evaluate the problem of freedom from contradiction in Leibniz's works, we are forced to admire the genius which was capable of recognising the fundamental problem at such an early stage. A deductive system must be proved free from contradiction if it is to be used for a purely logical structure. It is only through the studies which have been developed in our own century that we recognise the necessity as well as the difficulty of such a proof.

On the other hand, we must admit the validity of objections to Leibniz's basic pre-suppositions. Objections to a fundamental philosophical statement can be of different kinds. They can maintain that the statement does not fully apply to the phenomena which it is attempting to determine. This is probably true of every philosophical system and perhaps of every scientific statement. We should include under this heading Russell's objections to the analytic theory of judgement, to which we also subscribe. Leibniz's analytic theory of judgement sets out to be a general theory of judgement, but it does not succeed, for example, in embracing relative judgements, as these cannot be reduced to the form A is B. A similar objection could be made to the combinatorial theory of concepts, which by no means exhausts the totality of possible concepts, since there are other kinds of combination besides the additive which is here regarded as the only one. But probably a similar objection could be validated against every philosophical theory, indeed against any theory whatsoever.

There is another, and to my mind, weightier kind of objection, namely that which shows that difficulties and contradictions arise among the fundamental pre-suppositions of a philosophy and stem from the pre-suppositions themselves. This is true of Leibniz, whose pre-suppositions, as he is well aware, make it necessary to prove the freedom from contradiction of deductive systems, but such a proof is impossible under his pre-suppositions. The only proof allowed by Leibniz's pre-suppositions is the reduction by analysis of all compound concepts to simple fundamental concepts. Only such a perfect analysis would give a proof of freedom from contradiction, but for us, at least, such an analysis is unattainable. It remains a serious difficulty of Leibniz's philosophy that, with respect to the *a priori* systems, the only recourse for us at least is to experience and to factual existence.

CHAPTER VI

LOGIC

§ 18. A CRITIQUE OF LEIBNIZ'S LOGIC

To distinguish between an evaluation and an exposition of Leibniz's logic is basically impossible. To try to expound Leibniz's philosophy is an evaluation, and to make the exposition concentrate on logic and metaphysics constitutes a commentary. Nevertheless, a separate résumé of commentary and evaluation may not be without value.

What Leibniz says about the relationship of logic and mathematics has attracted particular attention in our own day. Bertrand Russell has emphasised the complete unity of logic and mathematics. The *Principia Mathematica* is constructed on this principle. It is clear that Russell is in complete agreement with Leibniz upon this point. Leibniz holds that logic and mathematics are one; such a view follows directly for instance when he treats the Euclidian doctrine of proportion as an example of purely logical forms. There are a number of places in which he expressly affirms the unity of logic and mathematics. He writes to Wagner:

'It is true that pure Mathematics is not logic itself, but one of its first offspring and is, so to speak, its application to quantities or number, measure and weight. I have also discovered that Algebra itself borrows its merits from a much higher art, namely, true Logic' (GP VII, 524).

In the first part of the Universal Mathematics he says:

'Arithmetic and Algebra can be so treated by means of logic, as if they were Logical Mathematics, so that in this way Universal Mathematics coincides in effect with Logistics and the Logic of Mathematics; hence our Logistics is given in some places the name, Mathematical Analysis' (GP VII, 54).

Kant's fundamental attitude brings him into opposition with Leibniz on this question of the relationship of Logic and Mathematics. Kant is constantly warning us that the various sciences should not be allowed to merge, but that their boundaries should be carefully observed. For Leibniz this is an almost incomprehensible pre-occupation. Working on this assumption, Kant drew a sharp distinction between Logic and Mathematics, a distinction which today we hold to be too sharp. Here, Leibniz shows a greater depth of vision. A system of logic which is sufficiently widely defined merges completely into Mathematics, but this view does not exclude the possibility of distinguishing the two disciplines. There is a similar link between mathematics and theoretical physics, but they can still be distinguished. The problem is made difficult by the need for new distinctions. Hilbert has drawn a distinction between mathematics and metamathematics and a similar distinction might be made between logic and metalogic. Aristotelian logic is seen in this light to be a complicated mixture of logic, metalogic and metaphysics, and Aristotelian metaphysics contains logical and metalogical considerations. I believe that the unity is stressed too strongly in the *Principia Mathematica* and too little attention paid to the distinctions for which there is a growing need. When, for example, we read in the *Principia Mathematica* that there must be at least one actual thing in the world, such a thesis can scarcely have a place in a purely logico-mathematical exposition. Among the aspects of Leibniz's thought which still, I feel, require special study is the *ars characteristica universalis* and particularly its implications for symbolic construction in analytical geometry. The continuous connection between logic and mathematics must be recognised but there is a need for new differentiations, which Leibniz recognised as pertinent but to which he paid too little attention.

The problem of the analytic or synthetic nature of mathematics is also one which is much discussed today. We have seen that Leibniz, in effect though not in his terminology, treated mathematical judgements as analytic and that this analytic theory can be summarised in the thesis: 'In every true proposition the predicate is part of the subject.'

Here, too, we find a decided difference between Kant and Leibniz. Kant's definition of analytic judgements corresponds to Leibniz's general definition of judgement; synthetic judgements are defined negatively: judgements which are not analytic are synthetic. In Kantian terminology it may be said that Leibniz regards both logical and mathematical judgements as analytic, whereas Kant sees logical judgements as analytic but mathematical ones as synthetic.

In his book on Leibniz, Couturat refuses to adopt a definite attitude to Leibniz's theory of analytic judgements. However, it can be seen from the way he writes his exposition and from later published work that he regards Leibniz's theory of judgement as objectively correct. On the other hand, Russell rejects the claim to exhaustiveness made for the theory of analytic judgements, and we hold Russell's view to be correct. Kant in my opinion underestimated the possibilities of logic in restricting himself to the syllogistic method in the narrowest sense. Had he seen the full possibilities of logic as Leibniz did and had he been consistent, Kant would, I believe, have described logical judgements as synthetic.

There seems to be little connection between Leibniz's theory of analytic judgements and modern theories, in which the definition of analytic judgements differ so widely from Leibniz that they seem to have little in common but the name. Leibniz's work can only be made to contribute to the technical problems of today if the connection with his definitions is re-established.

There is a somewhat more favourable position with regard to the problem (also intensively discussed at the present time) of whether *a priori* elements are present in science and particularly in the natural sciences, and if so, what they are, though we are admittedly faced with a diversity of definitions of the term *a priori*. However, all definitions agree at least in the negative thesis, that scientific statements do not consist exclusively of empirical statements, but that other elements are present in them and that these elements, however diversely they are defined, are *a priori* elements.

Leibniz maintains a decisively *a priori* point of view, even in his terminology:

'When however these things have been decided, they can derive all the phenomena of earthly things from these principles and, as they say, *a priori*' (GP IV, 257).

In this sense logic, arithmetic and geometry are for Leibniz an *a priori* of all science and especially of the natural sciences. As they derive from the principle of contradiction alone, they are, as we have seen, the only possible systems. Three-dimensional Euclidian geometry is, for example, the only possible geometrical system. From this there follows the unconditional and *a priori* validity of logic, arithmetic and geometry first for divine thought, secondly for the world as a reality created by God and thirdly for all knowledge of the real world and the possible worlds. Although we cannot entirely agree with his reasoning, I believe that Leibniz is substantially correct. His method is also a most interesting one for us. We tend at present to regard the *a priori* problem from the point of view of the causal law and the argument is almost entirely concerned with the question of whether the causal law is *a priori* or not. Leibniz states the problem in a better form when he says that it should be reduced to the question of whether logic, arithmetic and geometry are an *a priori* of science, and here it would probably be most promising to ask first of all whether the arithmetic of the natural numbers is *a priori* in character. Leibniz may have gone too far in his reasoning, but we cannot deny that statements about natural numbers are of a different nature from statements about the shape of the earth or statements about the deviation of magnetic needles (two problems with which Leibniz concerned himself). No one can be prevented from calling the judgement 7 plus 5 = 12 an empirical judgement, but in that case we should have to define the term empirical judgement so widely that the thesis would for all practical purposes lose its point—at any rate, the evident difference between the proposition 7 plus 5 = 12 and the declination curves of magnetic needles would disappear. I believe therefore with Leibniz, that it makes good sense to talk of logic, arithmetic and geometry as an *a priori* of the natural sciences, and I believe that the method of starting from these three disciplines is a good one.

We shall turn to three problems which can be regarded as having been acute at all times. The first is the question of the being of concepts. Here Leibniz was firmly of the opinion that concepts exist in themselves and was just as firmly opposed to the idea that we create concepts. Words and symbols emanate from us and are subjected to our free will, but the ideas which the words and symbols designate exist independently of us. It has become customary to express this by saying that ideas exist of themselves (or by speaking of the *Ansichsein* of ideas). The re-introduction of the ancient Platonic term, for this is in fact what it amounts to, does not seem wrong to me and I am therefore using it here, even though it is not normal Leibnizian phraseology.

This *Ansichsein* of concepts can be considered from two points of view, from the logical and the ontological. Under the logical heading the discussion concerns the logical structure of concepts which exist of themselves, under the ontological the question has to be asked, whether and to what extent his interpretation of *Ansichsein* as divine thought can be considered justified. We shall investigate for the moment only the logical questions; the ontological questions will be discussed in Part II.

Maintaining the *Ansichsein* of concepts generally leads people to maintain the existence of the totality of all concepts. Leibniz does this. In many places he mentions that the *scientia generalis* or the *ars characteristica universalis* makes it possible to present the totality of all concepts systematically. A typical passage occurs in the letter to Duke John Frederick quoted above.

The existence of such a totality of concepts is required by the combinatorial theory of concepts; in spite of this I have the impression that Leibniz approaches the problem with a certain degree of caution. He avoids actually giving the table of simple fundamental concepts, despite the fact that the totality of all concepts flows essentially from the totality of fundamental concepts. Further Leibniz specifically avoids all expressions which would denominate the totality of all concepts, such as *omnitudo omnium idearum*, or *totalitas omnium idearum*. It is possible that the objections to the concept of totality which he had noticed early prevented his doing this (GM I, 85). Leibniz liked to use the term *regio* or *région* which Lambert translates as 'the realm of eternal verities', and this translation, which I regard as particularly apposite, brings out the totality involved in the concept. Thus, in Leibniz's work, the problem remains ambiguous; on the one hand, his fundamental principles call for a totality of concepts, whilst on the other he obviously prefers caution. Certainly, he is not as clearly aware of the difficulties inherent in the idea of the totality of all concepts as we are today, and it is equally certain that it is intuition that makes him cautious. The difficulties which he saw intuitively—we may perhaps recall the concept of the *numerus numerorum*—have today become fully effective and raise objections which must be applied to Leibniz himself. All statements in his work which pre-suppose the totality of all concepts must be regarded with suspicion.

The possible contradictions in the totality of all true concepts require that the *Ansichsein* of concepts should be treated with a degree of caution, the necessity of which Leibniz may have felt intuitively, but which he was neither ready nor able to exercise. In any case, we must bear in mind that, even though today we are aware of these difficulties, we have yet to find a really satisfactory solution to them. Leibniz's over-optimism and his over-simple procedure were bound seriously to endanger the thesis in the form in which it was presented.

In my opinion, Leibniz sees the relationship between concepts in a much too simple light. In his theory of concepts and in his theory of judgement, Leibniz is aware only of combinatorial juxtaposition, that is of more or less additive combination, according to the model *animal rationale*. According to his theory all compound concepts must be built up on this structure. Yet there is no doubt that Leibniz himself employed quite different methods of compounding concepts. When, for example, he defines 2 as $1 + 1$, the two units which are contained in the number can in a sense be regarded as partial concepts, but they are not partial concepts in the same sense as *animal* and *rationale*. If the two were simply *unum, unum*, then this could be reduced, according to the law of tautology which Leibniz had already given, to *unum*; somehow or other the concept of addition must also enter into the definition. Basically, Leibniz makes use of the old Platonic notion of the pyramid of concepts in his combinatorial theory. Although Plato gives examples of such pyramids in the *Sophist* he shows in the same dialogue that other forms of relationship between concepts are possible, and himself uses the symbol of a net for the relations between the five fundamental concepts. We cannot then speak of a proper pyramid of concepts in the works of either Plato or Leibniz, as such an idea pre-supposes the existence of a single, highest concept. Nevertheless, if we wish to retain this symbol, we shall have to entertain certain serious objections to the idea that all concepts are on one level only and can only combine in one single way. If we wish to retain the spatial metaphor we must insist that the relationship between concepts is a stratified one and that in every stratum many forms of combination are possible.

A further objection must be raised to the idea of the precise definition of all concepts. There is, as Leibniz has pointed out in the *Meditationes*, a *notio perfectissima* for every concept, which is at the same time, a *notio intuitiva*. The basis of such a *notio perfectissima* is that the analysis of a concept is carried right down to the fundamental concepts which it contains and is therefore, as a general rule, unattainable by us. No one can doubt that the old Aristotelian judgement, which Leibniz consciously adopted, is the right one: 'not everything can be defined.' Leibniz remains curiously ambivalent in his attitude to this problem. If we had a complete analysis and a complete table of fundamental concepts we should at the same time have an exact definition of every compound concept, which means that for every concept of this sort there is an exact definition, a *notio perfectissima*, but as human beings we are not in possession of it.

Leibniz's caution suggests the presence of difficulties and here too his optimism probably goes too far. Whitehead, for instance, holds that exact definition is not possible even for the simplest arithmetical concept. Heinrich Scholz on the other hand seems to have been particularly attracted by Leibniz's idea that all concepts are capable of exact definition, even if their definability is only in themselves (*an sich*). We must interpret his view that logic can be made completely precise, in Leibnizian terms, in this light. Scholz sees an ever-increasing logical precision the nearer we approach to fundamentals: Whitehead sees an ever-decreasing one. We could say for example that Scholz regards the number two as a precise, or at least unusually precise, definition and Leibniz's declared view would support him in this, whereas Whitehead regards the number two as such a fundamental concept that we here find ourselves on the borders of definability. Clearly our historical view of this will depend upon the theory which we adopt. Scholz and Whitehead are both acknowledged Platonists and if we consider Scholz's position to be the right one we must also ascribe this position to Leibniz so that Scholz's interpretation of the work of his great predecessor follows naturally. If, however, we regard Whitehead as being right—and I incline to this view—then there is a serious objection to Leibniz's fundamental principle. In this case Leibniz's caution in stating that the *notio perfectissima* is not to be attained by human beings is once again evidence of his intuitive sense of the correct solution.

There is, finally, a fourth objection to Leibniz's fundamental principle. The principle means, as we have shown, that everything depends upon concepts and their definitions. Judgement is robbed of its independence and merely degenerates into an explanation of the relationships between concepts. At this point we are faced with a problem which can be viewed from both the linguistic and the logical viewpoint. The relationship which Leibniz lays down between concept and judgement when stated in linguistic terms refers to the relationship between word and sentence. If we state that the concept is the true basic phenomenon and that judgement is merely a consequence of the relationship between concepts, we are saying at the same time that the word is the basic phenomenon of language and the sentence merely a phenomenon derived from it which results from the combination of words. This view is dubious from the linguistic and the logical standpoint. There is good reason for stating that the sentence is really the basic linguistic phenomenon and the individual word only a derivation. If we transfer this idea to the sphere of logic it would mean that judgement is the truly fundamental logical phenomenon and that the individual concept is only a derivation. It seems to us that the reasons in support of this viewpoint are so weighty that the opposite thesis supported by Leibniz can only be regarded with great suspicion.

We have, up to now, been concerned only with objections.

There are two points upon which Leibniz's logic can be unreservedly accepted. First, the idea that logic is a science which is constantly expanding and developing, a point of view which we have expounded in § 7. Logic cannot be confined to the *modus barbara* and the further eighteen conclusions of the syllogistic system in its most narrow form; it cannot be regarded as a closed science. Kant's support for the opposite point of view is one of the weakest points of his *Critique of Pure Reason*. Leibniz sees that it would be possible to construct a logic of relationships and develop formal logic by extending the formal treatment at the very starting point of logic. It could be maintained that Aristotle was aware of both of these problems, that of the logic of relationships and of formalisation. It may well be that the orthodox treatment of logic, especially in the Middle Ages, was too rigidly confined to the *modus barbara* and its connections, although there is a wealth of medieval logic which goes much further than this. This, however, is something which has only recently come to light and it is unlikely that Leibniz was familiar with it. Then again, there is a rich body of logic extending from Lull to Junius which was available to Leibniz and which he studied with the greatest interest. Leibniz accepted this preliminary work gratefully and devoted a large part of his life's work to the development of formal logic.

I find it hard to believe the allegation that Leibniz's work had no influence on the development of modern logic, and that his work only became known after modern logic had developed independently. We need a detailed investigation of his influence upon people like Schröder, De Morgan, Frege and Peano. His influence upon Russell is clear enough, but would nevertheless merit a separate monograph.

Finally, we can accept Leibniz's logic without reserve at one last point and this is where he states that all human thought has need of signs, a point which we discussed in § 13. If we take a broad enough view of the concept of signs and include in it the idea of language in general, we may say that this is one of Leibniz's most fruitful ideas and that this tenet holds great possibilities for us and for the future.

PART TWO
METAPHYSICS

CHAPTER VII

VERUM

§ 19. THE OBJECTIVITY OF TRUTH

DOES truth have an objective validity which exists of itself or is it dependent upon human statutes, perhaps even dependent upon the human will and its pleasure? On this much-discussed question, Leibniz was always a decided protagonist of objectivity. Truth exists of itself and is independent of human will and pleasure.

From the historical point of view, the problem resolved itself for Leibniz into a dispute with the English empiricists, Thomas Hobbes and John Locke. His opposition to Hobbes is expressed in the *Dissertatio de stylo philosophico Nizolii*, published in 1670:

'. . . Thomas Hobbes who I must confess seems to me a supra-nominalist. For not content like the Nominalists in reducing universals to names, he says that the truth of things itself consists in names and, what is more, that it depends on human will, because the truth depends on the definitions of terms and the definitions of terms depend upon the human will' (GP IV, 158).

His disagreement is clearly shown here in the use of the term supra-nominalist (*plusquam nominalis*). Leibniz resumes the dispute in the *Meditationes* (1684). Here he says of Hobbes:

'. . . who wished truths to be arbitrary because they depend upon nominal definitions, not taking into account that the reality of a definition is not in the will nor that it is possible for any ideas whatsoever to be combined with each other' (GP IV, 425).

We have considered the theoretical problem at some length in Part I. It appears at first sight that definitions are arbitrary, but this, in fact, is not so as we have to prove the freedom from contradiction of each definition. We have seen that fundamentally Leibniz maintains that there can only be one definition for any concept, but this is an ideal which cannot be achieved in practice. However, as each concept has to be free from contradiction there can be no question of pleasure or will in the definition and so the argument of the English empiricists falls down at this point.

There is also a second argument which Leibniz regards as invalid and this concerns the nature of signs, especially mathematical signs, a problem which is dealt with in the dialogue *De connexiones inter res et verba et veritatis realitate*. It is true that Hobbes is not mentioned by name in this dialogue, but he is clearly identifiable and is referred to as the *ingeniosus scriptor*. We may take as our starting point the pre-supposition that truth and falsity exist in things and not in thought. The difficulty then arises that thoughts need signs and that all proof depends upon definitions. Now, it seems at first sight that signs as well as definitions are arbitrary and that hence the truths which depend upon them are arbitrary.

A. 'Therefore the truth of such propositions depends upon the definitions.'

B. 'I agree.'

A. 'But the definitions depend upon our will.'

. . .

A. 'Therefore arithmetical truths pre-suppose some signs or characters.'

B. 'That is so.'

A. 'Therefore they depend upon the will of men.'

B. 'You seem to be practising some sleight of hand.'

A. 'These are not my own subterfuges, but those of an ingenious writer' (GP VII, 191).

Leibniz considers the argument drawn from the differences between languages. He points out that the Greeks, the Romans and the Germans have the same geometry in spite of the fact that they speak different languages. He then proceeds to the discussion of the necessity and significance of signs and thence to the objective reality of truth. We draw our conclusions with the aid of signs and use arbitrary signs for this purpose. However, our conclusions do not depend upon the arbitrary element in the signs, but upon what the signs stand for; thus we arrive at necessary truths in spite of the use of arbitrary signs. The relationships between the arbitrary signs reproduce the relationships between things, a point which is demonstrated by the fact that signs may be well or badly chosen.

'There is some relationship or order in signs which is present in the thing itself if the signs are well chosen' (GP VII, 192).

The fact that there are good and bad signs is now investigated from the point of view of its ontological consequences. In the paragraph on the *characteristica universalis* (§ 13) we discussed mathematical symbols. We may recall the difference between Roman and Arabic numerals and Leibniz's proof that the signs which he had chosen for differential quotients were better than Newton's. If there are such things as better or worse signs we must agree that there must be something which these signs represent in a better or worse fashion, so that what the signs represent no longer needs to be subject to their arbitrary nature. Thus it is not necessary that the arbitrary nature of truths should follow from the arbitrary nature of the signs which represent them—indeed the phenomenon of signs leads to the reality of truth.

This question of the reality of truth occupies a comparatively large part of Leibniz's work, especially his correspondence, for instance the letter of October 1682, to Jean Gallois (Ak. II, I, 529), and that of January 1678 to Henning Huthmann (Ak. II, I, 391).

The dispute with Locke which occupied Leibniz so intensively for so long also culminates in the question of the reality of truth. The first blows were struck in *Sur l'essay de l'entendement humain de M. Locke* a relatively short paper which Leibniz sent to Locke in the hopes that he would include it in the French edition of the *Essay*. Locke, however, quite understandably did not find the paper to his taste and did not fulfil Leibniz's wish. Nevertheless the reflections were published during Leibniz's lifetime in the *John Locke Epistolae* (GP V, 14 ff.).

The *Nouveaux Essais* as a whole are a polemic against the idea of the arbitrary nature of truth and Leibniz not only investigates Locke's grounds for putting forward such a view but also deals with the general problem. Truth does not depend upon the signs which we use, it does not even depend whether we are in a position to achieve it.

'Even that which we cannot ascertain is nonetheless determined in the nature of things' (GP V, 136).

The truth of true proposition does not depend upon the will or the arbitrary nature of men, and does not even depend upon the will or arbitrariness of God.

This is a question much discussed in the Middle Ages in which there appears to be a conflict between God's omnipotence and his omniscience. Is God's omnipotence so great that it is unbounded and does it then follow that God can determine all truths according to his will? Could God, for instance, have determined that $3 \times 3 = 10$, and is it now true that $3 \times 3 = 9$ only because God has determined that it should be? This is the example which Leibniz gives in § 187 of the *Theodicy* (GP VI, 228). The same would be true of the principle of contradiction. According to this view, the fact that two propositions which contradict each other cannot both be true is only the consequence of God's having ordained it so. He could just as easily have created a world in which two contradictory propositions are always true. In one sense Duns Scotus had already considered such a view. Leibniz ascribes such an attitude to Descartes. He finds it in Descartes' own work, in the work of some of Descartes' school and in the work of Pierre Bayle. He makes special reference to the latter's *Continuations des pensées diverses* (*Theodicy* § 185).

Leibniz regards such an attitude as completely erroneous. As we have seen, Leibniz's necessary but sufficient criterion of existence for *a priori* truths was the principle of contradiction. All combinations of concepts which are free from contradiction exist and no others; every proposition which results from them is true and no other. There is no place here for decisions, not even for decisions which spring from the will of God. But even in the case of contingent truths which concern the structure of the existing world, the decision of God's will is only concerned with the world as such and not with the true, contingent propositions which are valid in it.

The objective reality of truth, not only with regard to the will of man but also the will of God, is stressed in many places by Leibniz,[31] for instance in § 46 of the *Monadology*:

'Meanwhile it must not be imagined, as a few people do, that the eternal truths being dependent upon God are arbitrary and depend upon his will as Descartes appears to have held and after him M. Poiret.'

§ 20. TRUTH AS DIVINE THOUGHT

The objective reality of truth consists in every true proposition being constantly thought by God; this is how Leibniz completes his ontology of truth. Truth is divine thought. This is Leibniz's constant belief linking him with Plato, Plotinus, Augustine and Malebranche. In the *Theodicy* § 20, Leibniz speaking of the eternal truths says quite simply that they are 'in God's understanding'. In the *Monadology* § 43 he says:

'This is because God's understanding is the realm of eternal truths or of the ideas upon which these depend, and because without him there would be nothing real in possibilities and not only would nothing exist but nothing would be possible.'

Perhaps the most illuminating expression of this comes at the end of the *Nouveaux Essais*.

'But in reply we shall ask where would these ideas be if no spirit existed and what would be the real foundation of this certainty of eternal truths? This leads us to the ultimate basis of truth, that supreme and universal being who cannot but exist, whose understanding is in truth the realm of eternal truths, which St. Augustine recognised and stated in a lively form. And so that it shall not be thought unnecessary to go back to this it must be considered that these necessary truths contain the determining reason and the regulating principle of existences themselves, in one word, the laws of the Universe. Since these necessary truths are anterior to the existence of contingent beings it is necessary that they should be based upon the existence of a necessary substance. There it is that I find the original of the ideas and the truths which are engraved upon our souls, not in the form of propositions but as the sources whose application and occasions give birth to actual statements' (GP V, 429).

Leibniz's most succinct summary of this view is in a letter to Des Bosses of 5 February 1712:

'Hence God not only considers single monads and the modification of every monad but also their relations, and the reality of truths consists of this' (GP II, 438).

This view of truth as divine thought is Plato's doctrine of ideas in Augustine's interpretation. It is possible to doubt whether this view occurs in such a strict and exclusive form in Plato, but it cannot be doubted that Plato sees an essential connection between ideas and God so that Augustine's interpretation may be regarded as at least possible in Platonic terms. This is certainly Leibniz's view and in § 20 of the *Theodicy* which we have just quoted he refers to the *Timaeus*. He also makes express reference to this point in the *Epistola ad Hanschium de philosophica Platonica sive de enthusiasmo Platonico* which was written in 1707 and published for the first time in 1716. Here he says:

'Meanwhile many of Plato's doctrines are most beautiful . . . the intelligible world, which I also am accustomed to call the region of ideas, existing in divine thought. . . . The mathematical sciences which treat of the eternal truths, rooted in divine thought, prepare us for the knowledge of substances' (E 445*b*).

Leibniz greatly prefers Plato's doctrine of innate truths to the doctrine of the *tabula rasa* taught by Aristotle and Locke. What he asks for is a combination of Plato and Democritus:

'And so I think that Plato might usefully be combined with Aristotle and Democritus to produce a true philosophy'

and finally in this letter Leibniz makes reference to Augustine and Malebranche.

Leibniz's relationship to the works of Augustine is an extremely close one and could be based upon close textual knowledge (*Theodicy* § 284).

The relationship to Malebranche is equally close and Robinet collected the material in the readily accessible form which we have today.[32]

There are two papers which deal specifically with Malebranche, the *Remarques sur le sentiment du R. P. Malebranche* written in 1708 and first published by Raspe in 1765 and the *Examen des principes du R. P. Malebranche* written in 1711 and published by Des Maizeaux in 1720. Among the works which Leibniz himself published, the *Theodicy* contains specific references to Malebranche.

In his theory of ideas as divine thought Leibniz comes into conflict with a more far-reaching view which was held before him by some Scotists, perhaps even by Duns Scotus himself and later by Bolzano. Bolzano admits that all true propositions are constantly thought by God but he regards this constant thinking as being not constitutive for the reality of ideas any more than for the reality of truth:

'It follows from God's omniscience that every truth even if it is unknown to anyone else, indeed if it is only thought, is known to Him, the omniscient one, and is constantly present in his understanding. Hence there is not a single truth which is not known by anybody. This does not, however, prevent us from talking of truths, as such, in the concepts of which it is still not pre-supposed that they have been thought by someone . . . although all truths are at the same time known truths (that is known by God): thus the concept of a truth in itself is to be distinguished from a known truth or, as it is said, from knowledge.'[33]

Leibniz sums up the attitude of the Scotists:

'some Scotists believe that eternal truths exist when there is no understanding, not even divine understanding' (*Theodicy* § 184).

Leibniz on the other hand believed that all essences and especially all eternal truths had to be founded upon an actual existence, since only an actual existence is capable of bearing reality. Eternal truths are necessarily founded on divine thought as the actual existence which bears them.

§ 21. SOME OBJECTIONS

This view of truth as divine thought could be called a theological basis of truth, and in this Leibniz is very close to tradition. We cannot understand his work unless we are ready to follow his train of thought. Yost, in an otherwise valuable work, says that this determination of truth as divine thought is merely a curiosity.[34] Such a prejudice would from the outset block any fundamental understanding of Leibniz's thought. Not that we wish to deny that there are serious objections to a theological basis of truth. We shall confine ourselves to mathematical truths and ask whether difficulties arise if mathematical truths are regarded as divine thought.

From a purely empirical point of view, of course, difficulties do arise, as Leibniz saw in the work of Hobbes and Locke. If true statements, and this includes mathematical statements, are entirely empirical and if they are even dependent upon the arbitrary nature of our thought they can no longer be regarded as divine thought. It must not be forgotten, however, that the empirical attitude itself involves us in considerable difficulties.

Yet if we reject the purely empirical view of truth and take the standpoint of the objective reality of truth we still come to a point where it is possible to reject the theological basis of truth. The most obvious example of this is Kant. In his *Critique of Pure Reason*, Kant says quite simply that space only exists from a human point of view. From this it follows that all geometrical truths, which are interpreted as statements about space, can only exist from the human point of view. We can then say that the difference between Leibniz and Kant is that Leibniz regarded geometrical truths as divine thought, while Kant looked upon exactly the same truths as human thought. This change from a theological to an anthropocentric view of truth is perhaps the fundamental distinction between the two philosophers. Perhaps this accounts for the many changes of attitude which, according to his own account, Kant underwent during the composition of the *Critique of Pure Reason*.

This distinction has very deep roots and there are, in fact, considerable objections to the idea of the theological basis of truth, both on theological and philosophical grounds. Theologically, it seems to me that the idea of truth as divine thought must lead to the likening of man to God. Thus, if God is the first to think mathematical truths and if these truths are then thought by human beings, human beings must be thinking in the same manner as God and must, in a sense, become like him. In fact, if the proposition, $2 \times 2 = 4$ is taken to be a truth which is first thought by God and then by man, man must obviously be imitating divine thought and this can only mean that men think the same thoughts as God. Plato saw this and said that the understanding of truth meant growing like God (*Rep.* 500D). This is the origin of the idea which occurs in the works of Plato and Aristotle, that the perception of mathematical truths is a turning towards the true being and thus towards the perception of God. Leibniz also says this:

'It should not be thought disturbing that I have tried to explain these things by means of equations drawn from pure mathematics, where everything is in most beautiful order, and where there are ways and means of discovering this order by an accurate contemplation, by which we gain an insight into divine ideas' (*Theodicy* § 242).

Leibniz can even ask whether someone who does not believe in God can do geometry (*Theodicy* § 144).

The basis of this view is that the human *ratio* is the basis of man's likeness to God (*imago Dei*) at least according to the Christian view. Leibniz recalls this in a letter to Mariotte in 1676:

'In my opinion, the greatest thing a man can do for himself is to perfect his spirit which joins him to God, as far as this is possible, by the force of nature. This is quite reasonable since it is the principal part or faculty of man' (Ak. II, I, 270).

In the *Considérations sur les principes de vie*, published in 1705, Leibniz says quite explicitly:

'God is as a King and Father to those substances which have intelligence and whose soul is a spirit formed in his image' (GP VI, 545).

On the other hand it is hardly necessary to point out that this notion of growing like God will rouse objections from Christian

H

theologians; nor is the problem a simple one for the philosopher. Mathematics, as we know and practise it, contains structures which the theologian cannot accept as part of divine thought. Neither the idea of the necessity of signs, nor the discursive nature of mathematical thought, as such, is acceptable to the Christian theologian. We showed in Part I how convinced Leibniz was that the science of mathematics was bound up with signs; this we saw was also true of thought in general and so of language: in mathematics the problem culminates in the sign as such. In addition to this we are faced with the discursive nature of mathematical thought, of which the discursive nature of counting makes us aware at the very outset. We can absorb a small number at a glance, but a larger one must be fixed by counting. All proof is of a similarly discursive nature, for proof implies proceeding step by step from one proposition to another. Neither of these two mathematical structures can be regarded as divine thought and so it is difficult to see how mathematics as we know it can be part of this thought. For this to be so every sign and every element of discursiveness would have to be eradicated and after this it is hard to see what would remain.

It is significant that Leibniz himself was aware of these difficulties and frequently mentioned them:

'For the rest M. Bayle knows quite well that divine understanding has no need of time in order to see the relation between things. All rational conclusions are more eminent in God and there is just as much order among them in divine understanding as there is in ours. For God there is only one order and one priority, that of nature: we, on the other hand, are concerned with a priority of time' (*Theodicy* § 192).

In the polemic against Locke which is appended to the *Theodicy* he says:

'Actually, God makes no rational conclusions for which he has need of time, like us, in order to proceed from one truth to another. In the same way that he comprehends all combinations at once, so he comprehends all inferences and understands in a more elevated manner within himself all rational conclusions that we can make, and it is for this very reason that his wisdom is the most complete.'

From this follows the infinite disparity between divine thought and human thought to which Leibniz refers time and time again, for instance in the *Epistola ad Hanschium* (E 445*b*).

There are certainly no fewer objections to the theological viewpoint from the physical side. For such a view to be true every true physical perception would have to constitute an insight into God's plan for his creation. Leibniz states this view in the *Journal des Savans* in his article *Réponse aux réflexions*, published in 1697:

'If God is the creator of all things and if he is sovereignly wise, we cannot reason about the structure of the universe without entering into a view of his wisdom, just as it is impossible to reason about a building without entering into the intentions of the architect' (GP IV, 339).

The theological question receives special emphasis in the correspondence with Clarke (cf. p. 11 above). Although Leibniz and Newton differed on many points they agree about the theological interpretation of truth. When, for instance, they are discussing the question of the atomic structure of matter, Leibniz asks whether God could have created atoms, which from his point of view was impossible. Newton does not object to a question of this sort for, although he believes in atomic structure, his method of procedure is the same. Newton tries to prove that God could very well have created atoms. This not only means that Leibniz and Newton agreed that God created the world, for there is no doubt of this in the mind of either, it means that for both of them a true physical perception was not only a perception of how the world is really made, but also a perception of how God made the world. The result is that, for both Leibniz and Newton, a true physical perception is an insight into the divine cosmic plan.

It is impossible to say how we are to reconcile Leibniz's insistence upon the theological foundation of truth with the objections which he saw and expressed. In one sense these difficulties are present in the works of Augustine, where this view is to be found principally in the early works. In his later works Augustine seems to have been oppressed by the objections. Augustine says in one of his later works (*Sermo* 68, 5, 6): 'Say, above whom does my spirit rest? Above the humble and the peaceful and above him who fears my word (Isaiah, lxvi, 2). Peter feared the word, Plato did not: let the fisherman keep what the noble philosopher lost.' The contrast between the simple fisherman and the noble philosopher applies primarily to purely theological problems, but its bearing upon the foundation of theoretical truth in general cannot be neglected. But neither in the work of Leibniz nor of Augustine can I see how these two thinkers cope with the difficulties nor, indeed, how they could have coped with them.

CHAPTER VIII

BONUM

§ 22. METAPHYSICAL, PHYSICAL AND MORAL GOOD AND EVIL

Leibniz makes the traditional distinction between several types of good and several types of evil. In the Latin summary of the *Theodicy*, he says:

'Each is threefold, metaphysical, physical and moral.

§ 30. In general, metaphysical good consists of the perfection and imperfection of things even those which have no understanding. Christ said that God, the Father, took care of the lilies of the field and the sparrows and according to Jonah God takes care of the living animals.

§ 31. Physical good is concerned particularly with the advantages and disadvantages of intelligent substances, to which belongs *Malum Ponae*.

§ 32. Moral good is concerned with their vicious and virtuous actions, to which belongs *Malum Culpae*.'

This distinction between metaphysical, physical and moral good or evil is to be found in many places in Leibniz's work, for instance *Theodicy* § 209. We are here interested primarily in metaphysical good or evil. This consists of a *perfectio realitatis* or an *imperfectio realitatis*, a perfection or imperfection of being. There are, therefore, different grades of perfection or imperfection and thus different grades of reality and different grades of being. Since Leibniz regards the principle of continuity as universally valid, these gradations must be continuous. In the *Theodicy* § 31 he speaks of different grades of perfection. In the *Monadology* § 50 he says, similarly, that monads differ from each other according to their perfection: 'One creature is more perfect than another.' Perhaps it is no coincidence that this striking sentence appears in the *Monadology* for monads are the most instructive examples of the gradation of reality. Plants are more perfect than sleeping monads, animals are more perfect than plants and human beings are more perfect than animals. A being capable of reflective thought, in other words man, is more perfect than a creature which does not have this power, in other words an animal. Reality, therefore, is a quantity which can be graduated by steps. This is indeed implied in the idea of a most perfect being, *ens realissimum*.

'Hence it follows that God is absolutely perfect: perfection being in a strict sense nothing but the quantity of positive reality, setting aside the limits or boundaries of those things which have them' (*Monadology* § 41).

From this it follows that *bonum metaphysicum* always consists of a positive reality, however limited this may be, whilst *malum metaphysicum* can consist of a lack, a deprivation, a limitation. The *malum metaphysicum* of animals consists in their lack of the power of reflective thinking, and so the *malum metaphysicum* of animals has no reality of its own. Only perfection, at however low a level, is real. All errors and defects are merely something lacking.

This conception of *malum metaphysicum* as a mere deprivation and not as an independent reality is the only thing that makes a Theodicy possible. But it involves a consequential definition of *bonum morale* or *malum morale*. Evil, too, the *malum morale*, consists not of a positive reality but of a deprivation. Here Leibniz is directly following Thomas Aquinas. For him, too, evil is not a reality but a deprivation (*Sum. theol.* I q.48 a.1 and 2), and it is only on this ground that the transcendental philosophical principle: *ens et bonum convertuntur* is possible. Leibniz himself subscribes to this principle (*Discours de métaphysique* § 2).

The old question of the objective reality of good is self-explanatory if good is regarded as a positive reality. Good does not depend upon the arbitrary nature of man but is founded in things themselves. The question as to whether good and evil are dependent upon the free will of God was much discussed in the Middle Ages. Was God able to decide by his own free will that parricide is good, or is parricide of itself evil? Leibniz is of the same opinion about this question of the objective reality of good as he is about the objective reality of truth. In a letter of 1676 he writes:

' . . . In my opinion another and most grave and dangerous error is born, that Good depends upon the free will of God and not upon the nature of the thing itself' (GP IV, 258).

If good does not depend upon God's free will then it certainly does not depend upon man's free will, and so good is a reality grounded in the nature of things.

§ 23. THE WORLD AS THE BEST OF ALL POSSIBLE WORLDS

Leibniz never entertained the least doubt that the world must be understood, and can only be understood, as a divine creation. But, in this case, it must be good and it must be the best of all possible worlds, in so far as other worlds are possible. This chain of thought is the basis of the *Theodicy* and Leibniz states at the beginning of the work: 'God is the first cause of all things' (*Theodicy* § 7). The following paragraph draws the consequence:

'Now this supreme wisdom united to a goodness that is no less infinite, cannot but have chosen the best. For as a lesser evil is a kind of good, even so a lesser good is a kind of evil if it stands in the way of a greater good: and there would be something to correct in the actions of God if it were possible to do better. As in mathematics, when there is no maximum or minimum, in short nothing distinguishable, everything happens in the same way, or if that is not possible nothing at all happens: so it may be said in respect of perfect wisdom, which is no less orderly than mathematics, that if there were not the best among all possible worlds, God would not have produced any. I call "World" the whole succession and the whole agglomeration of existent things, lest it be said that several worlds could have existed in different times and in different places. For they must needs be reckoned as one world or, if you will, as one Universe. And even though one should fill all times and all places, it still remains true that one might have filled them in innumerable ways, and that there is an infinitude of possible worlds among which God must needs have chosen the best, since he does nothing without acting in accord with supreme reason' (*Theodicy* § 8).

The doctrine that the world is the best of all possible worlds has been repeatedly mocked and laughed at. Among the most witty attacks is, of course, Voltaire's *Candide*. Candide is an avowed disciple of Leibnizian philosophy, who arrives at a castle, falls in love with the daughter and has to flee with her. During their long flight, the young couple encounter every imaginable misfortune, but Candide refuses to be dismayed: this is and remains for him the best of all possible worlds.

This doctrine is the inevitable consequence of Leibniz's presuppositions, and Leibniz is not the only one to subscribe to it. Gottsched quotes Thales in the notes to his translation of the *Theodicy*, but this reference is now regarded as spurious. Cicero writes, '. . . *neque mundo quidquam pulchrius neque eius aedificatore praestantius*' (*Opera omnia*, Leipzig, 1827, 1175*b*).

The words of Genesis are decisive for the Christian religion: 'And God beheld everything that he had made: and behold, it was very good.' Augustine and Thomas Aquinas conceived these words as decisive and even Luther accepted them in his early *Interpretation of Genesis*.

We are far too prone to interpret Leibniz's philosophy as an outpouring of the optimism of the Enlightenment. Leibniz was able to find support from a historical tradition reaching back into antiquity. There can be no doubt that his attitude is consistent with the Christian tradition. However, I believe that the thesis '*omne ens est bonum*' can easily be traced back into Greek thought. Leibniz finds support for his system both in mathematics and in philosophy. The mathematical support comes from consideration of maxima, as mentioned in § 4.

As the quotation from § 8 of the *Theodicy* shows, Leibniz's first philosophical concern was the concept of the world. When he speaks of 'world' he does not refer to this world at a given time and in a given place, he means rather the whole course of this world, which we might call a cosmos. In the cosmos in which we live, many things might have been different from what they are. Political boundaries could have been different, there might have been a different number of universities in different places. Because of the way the world is constructed, it is not possible to change just one factor by itself. If, for example, we were to think of a frontier running along a different line, we should immediately be involved in a chain of further alterations, and the frontier could only be altered if this chain of alterations had already taken place. Leibniz mentions not only political and geographical factors but also physical ones. He started from the view (*Theodicy* § 7) that the distribution of matter could have been quite different, indeed that matter could have been distributed in an infinite number of different ways. We saw however in the first chapter that there are immutable determinations of this world and we have also seen how variable and invariable determinations differ from one another in respect of the principles of contradiction and of sufficient reason. There is a set of conditions which are necessary because their opposites—in Leibniz's view—embrace a contradiction and these must therefore be valid in every possible world. Logical, arithmetical, and geometrical laws belong to this series.

On the other hand, the laws of motion do not possess this unconditional necessity and from the point of view of the principle of contradiction, other laws of motion are possible. Thus there are other possible worlds with different but valid laws of motion (GP IV, 594).

In order to clarify further the concept of possible worlds one may ask how many substances exist. Leibniz was convinced that there was an infinite number of substances in the world, in other words, using the terminology of the doctrine of substance which we have still to treat, an infinite number of monads. But what of the question of possibility? Are there possible worlds which contain a finite number of substances, and moreover are there possible worlds which contain only one substance, which, in other words, contain only one monad? This question is important in some modern fundamental theories, and is discussed by Russell, Whitehead and Heinrich Scholz. What is Leibniz's position with regard to it? A world consisting of only one substance would be an almost unbelievable impoverishment compared with the plenitude of the actual world. Nevertheless, Leibniz does not appear to have thought that a world consisting of only one substance would be contradictory in itself, although it would be so wretched that he did not think it worth investigating the possibility. However, we must agree with Bertrand Russell when he speaks of such a world as being one which is possible for Leibniz.

Heinrich Scholz tried to establish metaphysics as a doctrine of necessary truths: in Leibnizian terms as a doctrine of truths which are valid in every possible world.[35] But there are two objections to this. Leibniz certainly regarded logical, arithmetical and geometrical truths as being necessitated by the principle of contradiction, and as valid in every possible world. However, in the light of our present-day knowledge, Leibniz was in error on this point, and the existence of non-Euclidian geometry shows that there are other possible geometries besides three-dimensional Euclidian geometry. We must therefore remove from this realm of Leibniz's necessary truths an area which has yet to be determined, and we must presumably face the possibility that not one single truth is absolutely necessary. In any case, the concept of absolute truth would have to be defined and it would then have to be proved for a particular truth that it was necessary according to the definition. Heinrich Scholz does not seem to me to have given such a proof in his work, and as long as this proof is lacking, we shall be uncertain whether metaphysics as a strict science is possible in the sense in which Scholz has defined it. Further Scholz's suggested definition of metaphysics would differ greatly from Leibniz's use of the term metaphysics. We shall return to this in § 40.

We have seen that the concept of possible worlds was important to Leibniz in physics, but its importance is naturally far greater in the empirical sciences proper. The facts with which history and geography have to deal could, generally speaking, all have been different. They all represent, if considered as different, other possible worlds.

The possible worlds differ from one another because different grades of reality appear in them. For example, a world which consists of an infinitely structured matter and therefore of an infinite number of substances contains more reality than one which consists of a finite number of atoms and therefore of a finite number of substances (Third letter to Clarke).

The possible worlds form a series depending upon the reality which occurs in them and this series is continuous and has a maximum. Only because there is a maximum—the best of all possible worlds—can one of the possible worlds be real. If there were no maximum of reality which distinguishes one and only one possible world then there would be no sufficient reason why God should have created this world and only this one, and without a sufficient reason God would have been unable to realise any world at all. It is one of the tasks of the differential calculus to determine the maximum of functions and so the best of possible worlds becomes in a certain sense, and here Scholz is quite right, a mathematical problem. 'When God calculates a world is created' (GP VII, 191), and the determination of the best of all possible worlds would be amost instructive example of this mathematical thought. Leibniz can therefore say:

'From these things it has already miraculously become clear how a certain divine mathematics or metaphysical mechanics is exercised in the actual origination of things, and the determination of the maximum takes place' (GP VII, 304).

CHAPTER IX

UNUM

§ 24. THE MODES OF UNITY

IN our attempt to present in this chapter the problems of unity and in the next the problems of being, we encounter in an acute form the difficulties of systematising Leibniz's philosophical thought. The problems of unity and of being are so closely connected that they cannot be clearly separated. They always appear together in Aristotle, Plato and Parmenides. These difficulties may well have stopped Leibniz from giving a systematic exposition of his philosophy. The one work which can most readily be regarded as systematic, the *Monadology*, is justifiably based upon the concept of unity. We try to put systematic considerations first in this book, but it is far from being a truly systematic exposition. If in our treatment of *ens* and *unum* we begin with *unum* it is only because this is a way to make what we consider to be the fundamental problems more easily approachable.

Investigations into the concept of unity start from the Aristotelian view that 'unity' is used with different meanings. Aristotle treats this in two very similar chapters of the *Metaphysics*. He distinguishes first between *unum per accidens et unum per se*. By *unum per accidens* he understands for instance the coincidence of two accidents in one subject. In *unum per se* he distinguishes four meanings. The unity of mere coherence, the unity of form, the unity of the living individual, and the unity of the universal (*Metaphysics* X, 1; 1052a29, and V, 6; 1015b16). It is important to Aristotle to distinguish between unities which are contrived by man—those things which are nailed, bound or stuck together—and unities which exist in nature. Leibniz may have learned this method of analysing the meaning of unity from the textbooks of the day, but one would like to think that the study of original passages, especially of Plato, Aristotle, Thomas Aquinas, and Suarez was not less important for him. The influence of tradition on Leibniz needs to be investigated in individual monographs, which even today do not exist.

The problem of the universal comes under another heading for Leibniz. In the problem which then remains he distinguishes only two sorts of unity—unity as aggregate and unity as totality— *unum qua aggregatum* and *unum qua totum*.

'I also feel, having admitted substances beyond monads or having acknowledged a certain real unity, that unity which contrives that an animal or any organic natural body is a substantial unity having one dominant monad, is quite different from the unity of a simple aggregate, like a heap of stones; the latter consists of a mere local unity or unity of presence, the former of a unity constituting a new substance, which the Schools call *unum per se*, whilst they call the other *unum per accidens*' (letter to Des Bosses of 20 September 1712, GP II, 457).

Nevertheless, the distinction between *unum per accidens* and *unum per se* is not entirely the same as in Aristotle. A pile of stones constitutes a *unum per se* for Aristotle even though it is the lowest possible form of unity. In any case the Aristotelian sense of the *unum per accidens* cannot exist for Leibniz since, as we shall see, as far as he is concerned it is impossible for one substance to have two different qualities of absolute reality. Thus for Leibniz there are only two sorts of unity—*unum per se*, the individual living creature, and *unum per accidens*, the aggregate.

There is a discussion of this subject in the *Nouveaux Essais*. Here, under the title *On Compound Ideas*, Leibniz summarises Locke's view by saying that there are ideas of individual substances, the idea of a human being, the idea of a sheep. There are also ideas which are based upon the joining together of many substances, for example the idea of an army of men, or a flock of sheep. Leibniz says of this:

'This unity of the idea of aggregates is very true, but basically it must be admitted that this unity of collections is nothing but a relationship which has its foundation in each one of the substances separately. Thus, beings by aggregation have achieved no other unity than a mental one; and in consequence their entity is in some way mental, or a phenomenon like a rainbow' (GP V, 133).

This doctrine of the two types of unity becomes clearer if we break it down into individual questions. Aristotle distinguishes between a unity which merely belongs together and a unity which derives from a determinate form. He accepts something made by a craftsman as having this second form of unity. Leibniz on the other hand regards an artefact, no matter how artistically made and how finished its form, as an aggregate. In the *Eclaircissement* published in the *Journal des Savans* in 1696, Leibniz states that the unity of a clock is not the unity of a living creature. Only the unity of a living creature is a true unity, the unity of a clock is on the other hand only the unity of a mere composition: '. . . the unity of a clock is merely that of an assemblage' (GP IV, 494).

There is a significant difference between Leibniz and Aristotle in their view of the unity of the universe. Aristotle sees the universe, the cosmos, as a true unity, indeed it is the prototype of a unity (*Metaphysics* X, I; 1052a28). This is because the universe is a living creature to Aristotle, a view which is almost impossible for us to appreciate. Leibniz, on the other hand, can regard it either as the totality of living beings or monads, or as a purely mechanical system; in both cases the world is nothing but an aggregate. '*Praeter Mundum seu Aggregatum rerum finitarum* (Beyond the world or the aggregate of finite things)'—this is the beginning of the manuscript first published by Erdmann, entitled *De rerum originatione radicali* (GP VII, 302); and again in the *Nouveaux Essais*: '. . . The universe itself could not pass as a unit, as I have shewn elsewhere' (GP V, 138).

The same condition applies to infinite quantities; they are always aggregates and never unities.

'Meanwhile I feel, strictly speaking, that the infinite which consists of parts, is neither a unity nor a whole, nor is it to be regarded as a quantity except through a mental fiction' (GP II, 314).

Leibniz uses the principle that infinite quantities have no true unity to solve many of the difficulties that they raise. It may be assumed that Kant's doctrine of the antinomies was influenced by Leibniz.

Finally, the unity of inorganic matter is also a unity of aggregates:

'I do not think that there is more substantial unity in water than in a shoal of fish swimming in the same pond' (GP II, 300).

Thus the unity of the living creature must be regarded as the proper and only unity. All other unities are merely a *unum per accidens*.

§ 25. THE MONAD IS THE ONLY TRUE UNITY

The different sorts of unity differ from each other in that they represent unity in a proper or an improper way. Aristotle suggested this way of distinguishing them, and it becomes completely clear when Leibniz recognises only two contrasting types of unity, the unity of a whole and the unity of an aggregate. The unities which are only aggregates cannot be regarded as unities in the full sense of the word; only the unities which are wholes are unities in the full and proper sense.

Leibniz regards living creatures as the only unities which are wholes, and he uses for them the term *monads*.

We are now faced with the question of the extent and structure of the world of monads. I am the original image of the monad in the full extent of my own being. Here the fundamental features of monads are immediately recognisable: the monad is a thinking being characterised by *perceptio* and *appetitus*; the monad has a body. On this basis three realms of living beings can be counted among the monads: human beings, animals and plants. This section of the world of monads already forms a series containing an infinite number of monads, which are ordered continuously according to their *esse bonum* and their reality. Animals are more real and therefore better than plants, human beings are more real and therefore better than animals, as we saw in the previous chapter. This series continues upwards in the inhabitants of happier stars, who are more real and better than the inhabitants of this earth: it continues through the angels and finally reaches its conclusion in God as the *ens realissimum*. However, God cannot be termed a monad in every sense of the word. As He has no body He is, at least, a monad *sui generis*.

The question of how far the world of monads stretches downwards is harder to answer. Leibniz raised the question himself by talking of naked or sleeping monads (*Monadology* § 24). What are we to understand by this? Hegel distinguishes between inorganic, organic and conscious monads. Inorganic monads, according to Hegel himself, would be pure liquids, and according to the passages quoted by him the four elements, salts, minerals and metals.[36] Monads would be the inorganic substances in so far as they have a particular structure, but even in those passages cited by Hegel, Leibniz does not actually say that these substances should be monads. On the contrary he rather takes the point of view that they do not represent a *unum per se*. They are then only a *unum per accidens*, they are mere aggregations, and therefore in my opinion they cannot be monads. We should therefore stick to Leibniz's repeated statements that only organic living creatures can be monads.

What then are the sleeping monads? This can perhaps best be explained by saying that there is no minimum to the downward extent of the monads. Leibniz knew that there were infinite series which have no maximum or no minimum. Thus the real fractions $\frac{1}{2}$, $\frac{1}{3}$, $\frac{1}{4}$ . . . form an infinite series but as the smallest fraction does not exist, the series has no minimum (GP VI, 578). If this is the case then the sleeping monads are to be found at the lower end of a descending series. If this series has no minimum then the question of the lowest monad would be hard to answer. Leibniz expressed himself in this sense in a letter to Bierling (1711):

'Thus the monad . . . is . . . either primitive, namely God . . . or derived, namely the created monad, and it is either possessed of reason (*mens*), or sense (*anima*), or of some inferior grade of perception and appetition, analogous to *anima*, which is content merely with the name of a bare monad, since we do not know its various gradations' (GP VII, 502).

Unity is the fundamental feature of the monad. For this reason the *Monadology* begins with the statement:

'The monad is nothing but a simple substance, which enters into compounds: by simple is meant without parts.'

The concept of the aggregate is immediately contrasted with this concept.

'And there must be simple substances, since there are compounds; for a compound is nothing but a collection or *aggregatum* of simple things.'

The same thought is expressed, perhaps even more sharply, in the first paragraph of the *Principles*:

'Substance is a being capable of action. It is either simple or compound. A simple substance is one which has no parts. The compound is an assemblage of simple substances or monads. Monad is a Greek word, which means unity, or that which is one.'

If unity is the fundamental concept of the doctrine of monads and we obtain the fundamental concepts of the doctrine from within ourselves, then we must also be able to obtain the concept of unity from within ourselves. Man is the proper unity and in fact Leibniz says: '. . . man is a *unum per se*, a being endowed with a veritable unity' (GP V, 297). He goes on to say that I myself am the proper unity and that I derive the concept of unity from within myself. We have already met this thesis in the doctrine of innate concepts, and we can now see that for Leibniz the theory of concepts and the doctrine of monads form a complete unity.[37]

§ 26. THE ONTOLOGICAL PROBLEMS OF UNITY

Aristotle held, and we may still agree, that the old dual question: What is unity? What is being? is the question which is at once the most difficult and the most far-reaching in the whole of philosophy (*Metaphysics*, III, I; 996*a* ff.). These two questions being ever-present, it will be hard to avoid the danger of repetition in trying to investigate the historical antecedents of the question of unity in Leibniz's work.

The question of unity, in one of its senses, stands at the beginning of philosophy as we know it. The Greek natural philosophers can be understood in this light, as Aristotle was well aware. When Thales says 'Everything is water' he must also mean to say: 'Everything is One, namely water.' The unity of the world is thus seen in one particular element—water. We may therefore imagine that the natural philosophers were looking for the unity of the world. Parmenides found the pure form of expression for it. He talks of being itself, and unity is among the determinations by which he characterises being. Being is unity. Fundamentally this is only the pure expression of what the earliest philosophers thought, but in this pure form a difficulty already arises. Plato was the first to analyse this difficulty and it is not chance that the dialogue in which he does this bears the name of Parmenides. The difficulty, subtle as it is, can be reduced to one simple question: if being is simple does not the difference between being and unity introduce a plurality into being? In other words, is being not multiple simply because it is a unity?

It cannot be denied that the *Parmenides* presents almost insuperable difficulties of interpretation. At many points Plato plays an insolent game with the logical difficulties. He puts the patience of the most patient interpreter to a severe test. We are often in doubt as to whether there is a serious basis to his game, and many interpreters have sought refuge in declaring that the dialogue is not meant to be taken seriously. Nevertheless, I do not think that it is quite inaccessible if it is taken in connection with the *Sophist*. Leibniz spent a lot of time in the study of Plato, whose dialogues he read in the original. His work on the *Phaedo* and *Theatitus* was published in 1857.[38] We can also assume that Leibniz considered the *Sophist* and the *Parmenides*.

The question which Plato is discussing in the *Parmenides* is, I think, the following: How are we to understand the statement that something is a unity? Is being a unity a real property, and, if it is, how are we to understand the reality of this property? If 'being a unity' is not a real property, what is it then, how are we to understand such a statement? For that matter we shall probably do the *Parmenides* justice if we regard it as an aporetic discussion, with no unequivocal outcome; the doctrinal interpretation of Plotinus and of those interpreters who follow him, probably goes further than Plato's intentions.

It may now be clear why Aristotle regards unity as the fundamental theme of metaphysics. Aristotle recognises the special

position of unity in the same way as he recognises the special position of being. If we consider unity as a general concept, it is a
special sort of concept and not a genus concept. If we regard unity
as a property of an individual being it is a property of a special
type, and not an *accidens* (*Metaphysics* X, 2; 1053-4). The unity of
an individual being may be a property in a sense which has yet to
be determined, but in any case it is not a quality, it is not an
accidens, it is not an absolute reality.

Medieval philosophy develops the Aristotelian notion that
unity is not an *accidens*. Thomas Aquinas is the first to work out a
doctrine on this subject. He subsumes *ens*, *unum*, *bonum*, *verum*, and
later on one or two other terms, under the heading of transcendentals and distinguishes them from accidentals. Whilst an *accidens*, for example a quality, always represents a particular newly
added reality—a *res addita*—this particular reality is not present in
transcendental determinations, particularly unity. Unity as a
transcendental determination is not an additional reality, it is not
a *res addita* (*Sum. theol.* I q.11 a.1). The same problem can be
expressed in another way by saying that first with Aristotle
and then with ever-increasing consciousness throughout the
Middle Ages questions had been asked as to the sense and
meaning of reality. In what sense can an *accidens* be called real
and in what sense can a transcendental determination be called
real?

In the development of this chain of thought, Thomas Aquinas
distinguishes between two types of reality, predicamental reality
and transcendental reality, unity as *accidens* and unity as a transcendental, so that now these two types differ as to their kind of
reality. Duns Scotus affirms the distinction and is the first to fix
it both terminologically and systematically. Ockham on the other
hand regards such a distinction as unnecessary: his view is that
every real unity is a transcendental unity, so that it is neither possible nor necessary to distinguish between a unity which is predicamental and one which is transcendental.[39] This somewhat subtle
point of view makes an understanding of the subject rather difficult. If Ockham and, later, Leibniz are to deny the reality of relation, Bertrand Russell, for example, finds the chain of thought

leading up to this quite incomprehensible. Yet it is not the intention of either Ockham or Leibniz to deny the reality of relation, but rather its reality in a very special sense, in the sense of absolute reality which has yet to be determined. The reality which in Thomas' work is attributable to the transcendental determinations is attributable to relation in both Ockham's and Leibniz's work.

There is an exhaustive discussion of this development in Suarez's *Disputationes metaphysicae*, and Leibniz probably became acquainted with the problem through this work, though he may also have studied many of the original texts of Thomas Aquinas, Duns Scotus, Plato and Aristotle. On the other hand there is nothing to show that Leibniz had read Ockham's works in the original, though their philosophical positions are very close, at least on those points where Ockham has expressed himself cautiously.

What does Leibniz have to say about the traditional problem of unity? First of all, we find the differentiation between different sorts of unity, which Aristotle was the first to teach—a distinction which belongs to tradition and which we have discussed in § 24. Leibniz, in his very earliest writings, shows that he was familiar with the ontology of Aristotelian and scholastic transcendental philosophy—what Kant calls the transcendental philosophy of the ancients.

The problem revolves around the thesis: *Unum transcendens non est res addita* (GP IV, 18). Shortly afterwards it is expressed by saying, 'unity follows entity in concept, they are the same in the thing' (GP IV, 24). Unity does not, therefore, add any new reality to the being to which it is added; it is only distinguished from being according to the concept, in reality it is identical with it. Leibniz takes this from philosophical tradition. The problem takes a new turn for him, which we shall discuss in the next chapter, in that he discards the concept of an accident in the sense of a reality distinct from substance, so that he cannot keep the scholastic distinction between the absolute reality of an accident and the modified reality of a transcendental.

The second fundamental thesis of medieval transcendental philosophy is: *Ens et unum convertuntur*. We find this form of words many times in Leibniz's work. Its fundamental importance for Leibniz is shown in a letter to Arnauld written in 1687.

'Briefly, I hold that proposition to be axiomatic which can only be said by difference of emphasis, namely that what is not truly ONE being is not really a BEING either' (GP II, 97).

This letter was written as Leibniz began to write his most original work, the *Monadology*, and it pinpoints the conviction which underlies the *Monadology*: the monad is constituted by its unity, it is only a being in as far as it is a unity. Monas means in Greek and for Leibniz 'that which is one'.

§ 27. OCKHAM'S RAZOR

Leibniz mentions Ockham's razor in *De stylo philosophico Nizolii*, an early work not published until 1770.

'The nominalists are those who think that all things beyond single substance are mere names, therefore they naturally reject the reality of abstracts and universals . . . . at last, however, the nominalist sect lay in darkness until at length a man of the greatest ingenuity and learning for that time, William of Ockham, an Englishman, a disciple of Duns Scotus, but soon his greatest opponent, suddenly resuscitated it . . . the general rule which the nominalists use is: "beings should not be multiplied more than necessary" ' (GP IV, 157).

Leibniz may have learned of the principle in the contemporary textbooks, but he certainly read of it in Suarez. Suarez refers to the Nominalist view in his *Disputationes metaphysicae* (*Works*, XVI, 533) when he is speaking of quality. Here he says of the principles:

'The fundamentals of this view are that the distinction of things should not be introduced or asserted without cogent reason or necessity.'

There is a discussion of the question whether Ockham's razor is to be found in Ockham's own writings in Boehner's edition of the philosophical writings (Edinburgh, 1957, p. xx f.).

The positive meaning of the principle becomes particularly clear in the ontological problem of unity and, as in so many cases, the first discussion of the problem in Plato's *Sophist* (244B) is the easiest to understand. Parmenides had stated: 'Being is one'. But, asks Plato, what does this statement mean? If I speak of Cebes and Simmia, these two nouns each designate a separate being, for they are two names, but if I speak of being and unity, do these two nouns also designate two individual beings? If they do not, what do they designate? Or, to put it in another way, are both being and unity names? And if they are not—and we soon see that they cannot be—what, then, are they? It seems to me that Plato had already seen the problem very clearly when he puts the question, in the *Sophist*, whether and in what sense being and unity are to be considered as two beings?

There are difficulties in finding a suitable way of formulating the problem. From a purely linguistic point of view they are even greater for the Greeks than for us. We, at least, have two terms at our disposal, 'substantive' and 'name', but for what we here term 'substantive' Greek only had the term 'name'. The question which we have just formulated is thus impossible to formulate in Greek. If we choose the ontological formulation we find that the difficulties in different languages are of a different order. Greek has the extraordinarily flexible term τά ὄντα at its disposal, which can be translated into Latin as 'entia'. Scholasticism added the further term 'entitas'. Thus in both Greek and Latin the question can be expressed 'are *ens* and *unum* really two *entia*?'

The ontological problem of unity provides an instructive example of Ockham's principle. We may, perhaps, assume that not only is every substance an entity, but that every one of its characteristics and every one of its relations is also an entity. Whether this is possible or not and what Leibniz thought about it will occupy us in the next chapter. However, even if we regard a substance and all its qualities and all its relations as a multitude of separate entities, it would still not be possible to declare unity to be a further entity. True, substance with all its properties and relations forms a unity in actual existence, but if this unity were itself an entity, then it would only be one among the many entities to which it has been added, and so it would need a new unity in order to join this new entity to the existing entities; but this process involves a *regressus in infinitum*. This would be an impossible result, especially for the Middle Ages which held that there was only a finite number of entities in the world. This expression of the problem as a *regressus in infinitum* was well known in the Middle Ages, and it is to be found, for example, in the writings of Thomas Aquinas, but I do not know whether he was the first to develop the chain of thought along these lines, or whether it was known before him.

From all this it follows that we may distinguish being and unity, but that we may not assume two separate entities. There is only one entity, in general, a substance, and this entity, depending upon the view one takes, may be regarded as being or unity. To regard being and unity as separate entities leads to an infinity of entities. Thomas Aquinas uses the term '*res*' for what we here call entity and he can thus say of *ens* and *bonum* (where the same relation holds): '*Bonum* and *ens* are the same according to the thing (*res*) but different according to reason' (*Sum. theol.* I q.11 a.1). This is what Leibniz means when he says: 'Unity follows entity in the concept but is the same in the thing' (GP IV, 24).

As far as transcendental unity is concerned, therefore, Ockham's razor only expresses something which was well known to Aristotelian and Scholastic philosophy. To regard transcendental unity as a separate entity, as a separate *res*, means in fact, to multiply entities without necessity. The full meaning of the principle for Leibniz's philosophy will only become clear in the next chapter when we turn to his discussion of the reality of qualities and relations.

In his early writings Leibniz confidently affirms the principle, and can thus in a certain sense be regarded as a nominalist. We shall see that he did not depart from this fundamental attitude throughout his life (GP I, 56 and 98). Nevertheless, he later seemed to incline to a somewhat more considered attitude. At least this would seem to be the conclusion which we should draw from the way in which he treated the problem in the *Nouveaux Essais* (GP V, 303). It is relevant to recall that Leibniz was always a mediator; though the idea of mediation presupposes that he adhered to the principle of Ockham's razor, otherwise no mediation would have been called for.

CHAPTER X

ENS QUA ENS

§ 28. SUBSTANTIA: THE MONAD IS THE ONLY TRUE BEING

LEIBNIZ'S philosophy and his metaphysics culminate in the doctrine of monads and in this doctrine, too, the concept of being, from which everything else follows, is developed and worked out. A whole series of fundamental concepts are shown to be equivalent, in particular: *ens reale, unum per se, individuum, substantia, monas, animal*. The problem can be considered from the purely ontological point of view and it can also be investigated as a problem in the analysis of meaning.

If we choose first the purely ontological viewpoint, then the two concepts *ens reale* and *unum per se* are seen to be equivalent. Parmenides, Plato and Aristotle repeatedly considered the connection between being and unity. Transcendental philosophy in the Middle Ages expressed the relation in the proposition, *ens et unum convertuntur*, and we saw in the previous chapter that Leibniz was familiar with this expression. The connection between being and unity is the inescapable pre-supposition of every monad or individual living being. Whatever gains its unity gains its life and its being, whatever loses its unity loses life and being. Death is constantly called a loss of unity. Now Leibniz was convinced that in our world a living creature, a monad, can neither come into being nor cease to exist, at least not in the natural course of the world. It needs a special intervention of God to allow a monad to be created or to die, and for this reason the connection between being and unity becomes even stronger (*Monadology* § 4–6). Since a monad can never lose its life or being, it cannot ever lose its unity and its fundamental nature is to be a unity.

The second concept in this network of equivalent concepts in the doctrine of monads is the individual. Here we have the fundamental ontological thesis: only the individual, the individual living creature, has true being, everything else, totalities, universals, properties, relations only have a being which is based on the being of an individual living creature, a monad.

'For concrete things are really things, abstracts are not things but modes of things, however many modes are nothing else but relations of the thing to the understanding, or the possibilities of appearing' (GP IV, 147).

This principle that the individual living creature is real, that it alone—the monad—is real, and that nothing but the living creature is real is the true Aristotelian heritage in Leibniz's work. Aristotle says that substance is truly real and that substance in its primary meaning as *substantia prima* is always a τοδε τι (*Metaphysics* II, 5; 1001b32).

I do not know the details of the historical connection. Leibniz may have derived this thought direct from Aristotle or he may have found it in the work of Thomas Aquinas referring to Aristotle, or, again, he may just as easily have encountered it in the passage in which Suarez says: '*Unde D. Thomas. q. 9 de Potent. art. 1 ad 4 simpliciter ait, nihil subsistere, nisi individua substantiae.*' Lastly, he might have discovered it in one of the Aristotelian works of his own day.[40]

Bertrand Russell has paid special attention to the concept of substance, and we can base our conclusion to a large extent upon his investigations. Substance is one of the central concepts of metaphysics and attacks upon metaphysics usually focus upon the concept of substance, a not wholly unjustifiable procedure as Leibniz himself observed. In his *De primae philosophiae emendatione et de notione substantiae* which appeared in *Acta Eruditorum* in 1694 Leibniz admits that the essential concepts of metaphysics are obscure and ambiguous and he cites as examples: *substantia, causa, actio, relatio, similitudo* (GP IV, 468). This is directly contrary to the intention of Plato and Aristotle who both laid the greatest stress upon sound definitions. Their disciples were, however, more concerned with discussion and disputation than with good definition. In the *Nouveaux Essais* Leibniz attacks Locke on the question of substance. The idea of substance is not as obscure as we sometimes think and as Locke made it out to be. Leibniz summarises Locke's view as 'the words substance and accident are, to my mind, of little use in philosophy'. But Leibniz immediately replies:

'I declare that I am of a different opinion and I think the consideration of substance one of the most important and fruitful in philosophy' (GP V, 137).

The traditional definitions of substance contain three superimposed definitions. Substance is, first, the ultimate support of all properties and determinations, it is the *ultimum subsistens*. Secondly, substance is the basis which resists all changes, the *ultimum perdurabile*; and thirdly, substance is a being which has the origin of its activity within itself, it is the *vis activa*. Leibniz's goal is to demonstrate that the third definition is the true definition of substance.

In metaphysics in general, and especially in medieval metaphysics, the first definition is regarded as the decisive one. Substance is the *ultimum subsistens*. This may have two meanings, an ontological and a logical one. According to tradition, however, these are merely two aspects of the same thing. Leibniz, for example, says of the ontological definition that substance is the final bearer of all other properties:

'But there is heat or impetus in a body just as in a subject: and the final subject is always substance' (letter to Des Bosses, GP II, 457).

Leibniz talks of substance as the final bearer of all predicates in the *Discours de métaphysique* (GP IV, 432).

The second definition of substance designates substance as something which remains immutable in the face of change. Kant studied the difference between these two definitions. He showed that the difference is that time does not occur in the first definition, whereas it is added in the second.

Leibniz regards the third definition as the really fundamental one, and his treatise of 1694 concentrates upon this definition:

'So that I may give a specimen of this thing I will call it meanwhile the notion of force or power (what the Germans call *krafft* and the French *la force*) for the explanation of which I have destined the special science of dynamics, to bring more light to the understanding of the true notion of substance. For the *vis activa* differs from simple *potentia* which was generally known to the schools, which is nothing but the possibility of action, which is different from excitation and seems in need of a stimulus to be converted into action. The *vis activa*, however, contains a certain action or ἐντελέχειαν, and is a medium between the possibility of action and action itself, and involves an endeavour; and so is, of itself, brought into operation, nor does it need help, but merely the removal of hindrance' (GP IV, 469).

Leibniz underwent two changes of view in his early years with regard to the concept of substance. In his student period and for a short while afterwards we must regard him as a pure Aristotelian, with reference to this concept as well as in other ways. The *De arte combinatoria* (GP IV, 32) is an example of this. He then proceeds for reasons yet to be explained to a purely atomic theory, which means especially in physics a purely materialist point of view. The evidence for this is the long letter (GP I, 21) which he wrote to his teacher Thomasius and which he published in 1670 in the edition of Nizolius. This change-over to pure materialism must have involved a change of attitude to the concept of substance. In this period substances are atoms and empty space.

Leibniz probably arrived at his final concept of substance during his journey to Paris,[41] and he clings steadfastly to this concept. In his essay which appeared in *Acta Eruditorum* in 1698, *De ipsa natura sive de vi insita actionibusque creaturarum* he says, apparently with reference to his essay of 1694:

'To which may be added what I have said elsewhere though perhaps not sufficiently thoroughly for everyone, that the real substance of things consists in power of acting and of suffering' (GP IV, 508).

The *Principes de la nature et de la grace, fondés en raison* begin with the same statement: 'Substance is a being capable of action.' We find the same definition of substance in the *Theodicy* § 400 and in the *Réponse aux Reflexions* published in 1709 in the *Journal des Savans* (GP IV, 594). Leibniz says succinctly: 'Whatever is incapable of activity, does not deserve the name substance' (*Theodicy* § 393). Russell summarises this definition of substance in the term 'activity', but perhaps it would be even better to follow the example of the *Theodicy* and term it spontaneity. We could then say: Leibniz defines substance as that which contains the principle of its actions and passivity in its own spontaneity.

Three points can be made about this definition of substance as activity or spontaneity.

The first is that Leibniz expressly preserves the connection with the definitions of Plato and Aristotle. In a letter to Sturm Leibniz speaks of restoring the ancient and true philosophical definition of substance propounded by Plato and Aristotle (E 145*a*). Again in the *Theodicy* § 323 he emphasizes his connection with both Plato and Aristotle.

Leibniz may well have been thinking of the definition of being as *dynamis* in the *Sophist*. When in the *Theodicy* § 32 he acknowledges the term τὸ αὐτοκίνητον as coming from Plato, he is wrong, for the term does not occur in Plato but in Aristotle's *Physics* (VIII, 5; 258a2); however, the error is understandable as long as there were no comprehensive indexes to the works of Plato or Aristotle. The concept of αὐτοκίνητον does occur in Plato (*Leg.* X 896 and *Crat.* 399D). The quotation from Aristotle which occurs in § 301: 'that is spontaneous whose principle is in action' could refer to several passages, for example 324b13, 430a12 and 703a13.

We lack more detailed evidence of Leibniz's first-hand knowledge of the texts of Plato and Aristotle and this is something of which there is a great need.

The second point which may be made about this definition of substance as activity is that it is in complete opposition to Descartes. Indeed, it is possible that Leibniz's dispute with Descartes may have contributed to his arriving at this concept of substance. The differentiation between *res cogitans* and *res extensa* is not simply that *res cogitans* is a substance, for here Leibniz would be in complete agreement. It means more than this, it means that the *res extensa* is also a substance and this is the decisive difference between Leibniz and Descartes after Leibniz had recovered from his atomic period during his stay in Paris. Thus the essay of 1694 starts from a denial of Descartes. In the light of the new definition of substance as activity and spontaneity, *res extensa* cannot be considered a substance, nor did Leibniz think that it should be.

If, finally, we ask where is the concept of substance to come from? Leibniz answers decisively, as in his theory of concepts: from within ourselves. I myself am a substance and I obtain the concept of substance when I look at myself. Thus Leibniz in the *Nouveaux Essais* says:

'I believe that reflection suffices to gain the idea of substance within ourselves, who are ourselves substances' (GP V, 96).

The concepts of being, unity and substance are the most important examples of innate ideas.

The network of equivalent concepts includes the concept of the monad and of the living creature. The term monad is not found in the early writings and Leibniz may well have coined it between 1680 and 1690 or perhaps he actually adopted it from van Helmont as Stein has suggested. In the previous chapter, we demonstrated our conviction that Leibniz always thought of a monad as a living creature and that Hegel's idea that Leibniz recognised an inorganic monad must be rejected. Thus Leibniz writes to des Bosses:

'I restrict corporeal or composite substance to living things alone, or solely to organic natural machines. The remainder are to me only aggregates of substances, which I call substantiates, an *aggregatum* actually constitutes nothing but a *unum per accidens*' (GP II, 520).

He says the same thing in the *Monadology* (§ 63):

'The body belonging to a monad (which is its entelechy or soul) constitutes along with the entelechy what may be called a living being, and along with the soul what is called an animal.'

If we consider this as a problem in the analysis of meaning we find many problems in Leibniz's works which come under this heading. We may summarise the situation once again by asking: Where according to Leibniz can the meaning of being and the corresponding meanings of substance and reality be found? Leibniz's answer is unambiguous: from within me. I find my knowledge of the meanings of being, unity, substance and reality within myself. What does this mean? I think that what Leibniz is initially trying to say is that I am myself a monad and furthermore I am the original image of a monad. I know from within myself what a monad is with all the ontological and ontic determinations which belong to it. All this knowledge can be gained and can only be gained if I observe myself. This is true, first, of the qualitative determinations of monads, of *perceptio* and *appetitus* or, when it refers to human beings, of *apperceptio* and *appetitus*. I find out what *perceptio* and *appetitus*, intelligence and understanding, are when I observe myself and it is only in this way that I can find out. I myself possess intelligence and will and if I ascribe understanding and will to other beings, and the doctrine of monads ascribes *perceptio* and *appetitus* to all living creatures, basically I am only saying that they are similar to me. This is also true of the fundamental ontological determinations. I am a being, a unity, a substance, I am real. I myself am *ens*, *unum*, *substantia*, *realitas*, and I find them within myself. If I ascribe these fundamental determinations to other beings, and Leibniz ascribes them to all monads, then basically I am merely saying that they are like me.

Leibniz's firm belief that the fundamental ontological concepts cannot be derived by empirical experience from the world around us, but can only be reached through pure experience from within ourselves, links him truly to Plato. There is here, too, a true link with Kant's later thought. Cassirer's interpretation of Kant is made possible by this *a priori* concept of pure, fundamental concepts. Leibniz himself was fully aware that, in this question, he agreed with Plato and was in diametrical opposition to Aristotle. He expresses this opposition to Aristotle quite clearly in the introduction to the *Nouveaux Essais*. This does not in any way prevent Leibniz from agreeing with Aristotle about other fundamentals. Indeed, it would be a denial of his own fundamental synthetic point of view if he did not.

We can summarise the points discussed in this paragraph in the following way: That which truly exists, the *ens*, is a monad. The term 'truly exists' can be rendered as *ens reale* and the thesis can then be expressed: The monad, and only the monad, is the *ens reale*. The term *ens reale*, it is true, is to some extent a pleonasm, since the concept of *ens reale* is already included in the concept of the *ens*. Since however we have the terms *ens rationis* and *ens fictitium*, the term *ens reale* can be defended. The term occurs in Leibniz's works, in his first dissertation and in later writings.

All in all, the thesis that only the monad, only the individual living creature is an *ens reale*, leads us to the conclusion that the basic concept in Leibniz's work is individuality. This is so fundamental that it has always been recognised. F. H. Jacobi was probably the first to point it out. Schelling assents to Jacobi's interpretation in *Ideen zu einer Philosophie der Natur*. Hegel, too, in his *History of Philosophy* remarks upon it and summarises it by saying: Leibniz's fundamental principle is the individual. Heimsoeth describes Leibniz as the most extreme individualist in the history of thought. Kabitz pays particular attention to the problem of individuality in Leibniz's works, and Schmalenbach in his great exposition of Leibniz's philosophy takes individuality as his starting point. Finally, Mahnke clearly summarises what has been said on this question of the individual, as he does all other questions.[42]

If we look at the question from the point of view of the history of philosophy then we see that Leibniz agrees essentially with Aristotle, though it could be said that he presented the Aristotelian viewpoint in a more extreme form. Aristotle says that substance, in its true meaning, is the *substantia prima*, the individual, the τόδε τι, and that everything else which exists must have its foundation in the being of individual substance.

§ 29. QUALITAS

The monad is the only reality and all reality is contained in the individual living creature; Leibniz accentuates this thesis by denying true reality to everything else. We are all too inclined to see the negative part of such a point of view as merely being a dispute about the reality of universals. Of course, it is partly this, and this is the great difference between Plato and Aristotle. Plato sees the Idea, the Universal, as the only true being, the only thing that is real. Aristotle, on the other hand, only regards the individual in the true sense as real, and the universal exists only to the extent that it has its basis in the individual. The possibility of regarding general concepts as separate entities, is not, I think, really seriously considered by Leibniz, and on this point he is a complete Aristotelian. He considers general concepts to be divine thought, and this, he himself believes, makes him into a true disciple of Plato. On the other hand, I have found no passage in which he regards general concepts as entities, nor any where he polemicises against such an attitude. The struggle against the idea of entities other than the individual living creature is very important to Leibniz, but he sees it exclusively as a struggle against the view that qualities and relations, especially time and space, are entities. Neither quality nor relations are an *ens reale*, and Leibniz develops this thesis in a long argument against scholastic philosophy, an argument which is especially suitable for further clarifying the meaning of reality.

The scholastic view of quality, as Leibniz probably first encountered it, understands quality as a general concept and asks what kinds are included under this concept. In accordance with Aristotle four types of quality are distinguished. Leibniz may have met this usual distinction in the works of Suarez who says:

'Aristotle silently dividing quality in the predicaments names four types of it, each of which is twofold or binomial, habit and disposition, natural force and impotence, suffering and passive quality, figure and form' (*Disp. Met.* XLII, 2, 1).

A few traces of this initial, orthodox treatment of quality can still be found. For instance, in the letter to Wagner, which we quoted above, Leibniz writes:

'I found the greatest pleasure in the predicaments . . . I often asked myself and my fellow students to which predicament and which field this or that might belong . . . for one may only ask oneself or others about certain predicaments and their divisions (of which I have collated extensive tables from all sorts of works on logic)' (GP VII, 516).

The exhaustive tables which the boy had collated are apparently not the categories themselves, on which there could be little to collate, but the further divisions (like those which we have cited from Suarez) of quality into four species. Similarly in the early work, the *De arte combinatoria*, Aristotle's four fundamental qualities, warm, cold, damp, dry are classified as *qualitates primae* (GP IV, 45).

This early period is soon overshadowed by the change to atomic theory, which makes deep inroads into the Aristotelian doctrine of categories. Atomism only admits purely mechanical qualities, all other characteristics are mere phenomena. For this reason atomism necessarily distinguishes between primary and secondary qualities; only mechanistic characteristics in their function as primary qualities are real, and all other characteristics are merely appearances to a perceiving subject and are, therefore, merely phenomenal. Thus, from the point of view of atomism the problem of quality reveals itself as a problem of reality and we then encounter the question as to what we are to understand by the reality of a quality. The problem is complicated by the fact that different points of view provide different answers.

The Aristotelian scholastic point of view rejects atomism and embraces a continuity theory, though Duns Scotus is the first to express it clearly. It seems to me that Duns Scotus is expressing the views both of Thomas Aquinas and of Aristotle, even though the actual measure of agreement between Scotus and Aristotle must remain in doubt until we have detailed monographs upon the subject.

The scholastics interpret the reality of quality as meaning that qualities are separate entities which are distinguished by a *distinctio realis* from substance, from each other and from all other entities. I shall term this doctrine the doctrine of the absolute reality of qualities. It is to be found implicitly in the work of Thomas Aquinas, but it is left to Duns Scotus to provide it with a fixed terminology. Ockham retains it though not in its full extent, and Suarez as usual gives a reliable account of it.

Duns Scotus distinguishes three forms of being: *ens reale, ens formale* and *ens rationis*; *ens reale* and *ens rationis* constitute the original contrast between that which is real and that which is merely thought. The traditional examples of the *ens rationis* are the mythical beasts. Between the two forms of being Duns Scotus inserts a new form, the *ens formale*. Anything that is merely thought still belongs to the *ens rationis*, all substances and accidents belong to the *ens reale* and it is mainly the transcendentals which belong to the *ens formale*. Three differences of being correspond to

K

the three modes of being, an *ens rationis* distinguishes itself from another *ens rationis* and from its bearer (for instance, two different names for the same person and the person) by its *distinctio rationis*. A *distinctio realis* distinguishes two substances from each other, an accident from its substance and two accidents from each other. A *distinctio formalis* distinguishes transcendentals from each other—for example *ens* and *unum*—and from their bearer. Leibniz refers to Duns Scotus in his dissertation:

'(*distinctio formalis*) is attributed to Scotus as a medium between the real and the rational, whence its divisions are called *Formalistae*' (GP IV, 25).

Ockham takes up these terms but reduces them in extent. For him there are only a few qualities which represent an *ens reale*, which distinguish themselves therefore from one another and from their substance by a *distinctio realis*. He rejects the character of *ens reale*, and its determination by a *distinctio realis*, for quantity and for most qualities. He is therefore concerned in this argument with the further clarification of the meaning of *ens reale* and *distinctio realis*. According to this view the meaning of the two terms can only be determined from substances. A substance is an *ens reale* and two substances are distinguished by a *distinctio realis*. In this sense he understands an *ens reale* as an absolute which is really distinct from all other absolutes (*res absolutae*). Thus Ockham regards substance and real qualities as *res absolutae realiter distinctae* (*Sum. tot. log.* cap. 44). Kant's term 'absolute reality' is obviously closely connected with this. By 'absolute reality' I understand being as Duns Scotus ascribed it to substances and all accidents and as Ockham ascribed it to substances and some qualities.

It is essential for our present argument that this absolute reality should be ascribed to qualities, whether all or some of them. We are most concerned with the four fundamental qualities as described by Aristotle, cold, warm, dry, wet, in addition to which there are the colours. These four qualities and, generally speaking, the colours as well are each an *ens reale*, a *res absoluta realiter distincta* which is distinguished from its substance and from all other absolute realities by a *distinctio rationis*. This conception forms the doctrine of the *formae sensibiles* (*Theodicy* § 87). The reality of these qualities rests in their being separate *res*, and we have used the term entity in this sense.

The qualities which we have just enumerated form the kernel of the secondary qualities. Throughout his life, Leibniz was passionately opposed to the hypostasis of secondary qualities as absolute realities, although it is impossible to determine clearly his views during his early years as a student. He applies Ockham's razor against such a hypostasis, in spite of the fact that Ockham himself clung to the idea of the absolute reality of some of the secondary qualities. The connection with Ockham's principle is expressed in the *Confessio naturae contra Atheistas* which was written in 1668 and published in 1669:

'In rendering the reasons for corporeal phenomena neither to God nor to any other thing they have to take quite unnecessary refuge in form or incorporeal quality' (GP IV, 106).

Leibniz's argument against the absolute reality of secondary qualities begins in the period of his atomist beliefs. This is a remarkable, though short, interlude in Leibniz's development. We are unable to arrive at any conclusions about Leibniz's position on the basis of the *De principio individui* or the *De arte combinatoria*, but I assume that he adopted the Aristotelian views of his teachers. This interlude is followed by a brief, though energetic, atomistic phase in which he held that empty space is a substance and that atoms exist in a vacuum as further substances and are distinguished by size, shape and movement (*magnitudo, figura, motus*) (GP IV, 106 f.). This is the ancient atomistic programme, which was developed by Democritus, probably handed on by Gassendi and accepted by Leibniz with all the enthusiasm of youth.

Magnitudo, figura and *motus* are the only primary qualities which it is permissible to use for the explanation of nature. Shortly afterwards, Leibniz says, in a letter to Thomasius, which was published in 1670:

'For even if each explanation were possible, that of the scholastics and of the more modern philosophers, nevertheless of two hypotheses, the clearer and more intelligible should always be chosen, and I scarcely doubt that this is the hypothesis of the more modern philosophers which does not postulate any incorporeal beings in the middle of bodies, but assumes nothing other than size, form and movement' (GP I, 17).

It follows from this statement that no secondary quality represents an entity, but that they all can, and must, be reduced to *magnitudo, figura* and *motus*, as the primary qualities. This is particularly true in the case of colours. Leibniz gives an example of this in the whiteness of foam—he thinks of the surface of the water as consisting of nothing but small bubbles (GP I, 19). The *qualitates sensibiles* are nothing but a fiction (GP V, 363) and the only things which exist are atoms and their mechanistic determinations. In this struggle against the fiction of the *formae sensibiles* we see the beginning of the dispute between our modern era and the Middle Ages and Leibniz takes a most lively part in the polemics which form the background to the dispute.

Leibniz's view was that secondary qualities are mere phenomena, primary qualities are real. We might wish that Leibniz had expressed this idea a little more clearly and in order to do this he would have had to say what he meant by the reality of primary qualities. This did not happen because Leibniz gave up the point of view in the face of the beginnings of his doctrine of monads, where he interprets not only secondary but also primary qualities as phenomena. This second step is made plain in the paper which Erdmann first published, *De modo distinguendi phaenomena realia ab imaginariis*:

'I am able to prove that in bodies not only light, heat, colour and similar qualities are apparent, but also movement, shape and size' (GP VII, 322).

The point of view, which we have outlined above, that secondary qualities are merely phenomena and that primary qualities are real, involves a series of pre-suppositions only some of which Leibniz retains. It pre-supposes, first of all, that there is a distinction between primary and secondary qualities and Leibniz probably always subscribed to this view, even if it later lost significance for him. He finds such a distinction in Locke's works and expresses his agreement in the *Nouveaux Essais* (GP V, 117). The view further pre-supposes a purely mechanistic explanation of nature and Leibniz always agreed with this. In 1678, he wrote to Conring:

'Everything in nature happens mechanically, that is, according to certain mathematical laws laid down by God. I do not know why you count this among the most absurd things. I recognise nothing in things but minds and bodies, nor in minds but understanding and will, nor in bodies in so far as they are disjoined from minds, except size, form and place and their mutations in part or in whole. Other things are said and are not understood. They are sounds without meaning' (GP II, 197).

In the phrase *sunt sine mente soni* (they are sounds without meaning) he is clearly expressing his opposition to the hypostasis of secondary qualities. In the autumn of 1706 Leibniz writes to Des Bosses:

'It is true that all natural phenomena of bodies (with the exception of perception) can be explained by shape, size and movement' (GP II, 314).

He sums up the situation in a letter to Bernoulli: 'I have often stated that all things in nature are mechanistic' (GM III, 28). On the other hand, he soon gave up his atomistic theory in favour of the continuum theory. As we saw in Part I, Leibniz regards the actual world as being continuously filled with matter, whilst the atomic theory, if indeed it is free from contradiction, can only hold good for certain possible worlds.

This transition from atomic theory to continuum theory is bound to involve a change in the interpretation of primary qualities.

Whatever Leibniz's view of the possibility of an atomistic world may have been, in the real world matter is continuously distributed in space and this should be the first concern of physics and metaphysics. If we subscribe to the mechanistic explanation of nature, then matter, size, form and movement are mechanistic fundamental categories. Philosophy has to ask what meaning the reality of these fundamental categories can have. We shall see later that they are interpreted as *phaenomena bene fundata*, but in order to make this possible, the fundamental mechanistic categories have to lose their character as absolute realities.

In what sense can matter, size, form and movement be called real? If we consider the three last named then we are dealing exclusively with primary qualities. In Duns Scotus' scholasticism, in Thomas Aquinas, they are conceived as real accidents and as real qualities. For Scotus this means that they are *res absolutae realiter distinctae* and there are *formae sensibiles* which correspond to them; they are separate entities which are distinguished from their substance and each other by a *distinctio realis*. However, a categorial analysis of the problem, like that performed by Ockham, shows that this is much too simple a view. It seems to me that Leibniz's train of thought can be expressed in the following way:

Size is a quantity. Now, it is true that Duns Scotus had called quantity, or at least *quantitas continua*, a real *accidens*, but Ockham opposed this point of view. This means that the categorial independence of quantity is done away with and quantity is categorially subsumed under relation. We saw in Part I that Leibniz also did this. However, if quantity belongs categorially to relation then it is also subject to the ontological determination of relation and in the next section we shall see that relation for Leibniz had no absolute reality.

Motus, movement, disappears at the outset from the sphere of qualities. Upon a closer analysis, it becomes clear that this, too, is a phenomenon of relation and this is Leibniz's point of view.

The only thing left is form, which alone has any prospect of being determined as a real *accidens*. It is a real *accidens* to Duns Scotus and to Thomas Aquinas and, as both of these philosophers believed, to Aristotle, but this determination of form immediately entails difficulties, as Ockham quite clearly observed. If, for example, we bend a steel blade, its form is changed, it deviates from the straight into a curve of varying flexure. Now, if every figure is a real *accidens* then it would have to attain a new entity and lose its old one every time it was bent; but this flexure is continually happening, and it is scarcely credible that a steel blade should continually be losing real accidents and be attaining new ones (*Sum.*

tot. log., cap. 55). Leibniz gives another example. A body of soldiers performing drill movements can form itself into a number of figures: a square, a line, a rank, but it seems misleading to consider the rapidly changing figures as real accidents (*Theodicy* § 395). This example is apparently directly related to Leibniz's doctrine of the continuum. If matter fills space continuously forms and figures arise in it by means of a constant movement and pass away by means of a constant movement. In a continuous world there are no constant forms and figures at all, but everything is in a state of constant and continuous motion. There is, therefore, no basis for ascribing real accidents to the figured matter which is in a state of constant motion. Therefore, after Leibniz has subscribed to the determination of secondary qualities as mere phenomena, the primary qualities now lose their being as absolute reality and appear as mere phenomena. From this we can see the justice of the passage which we quoted above:

'I am able to prove that in bodies not only light, heat, colour and similar qualities are apparent, but also movement, shape and size' (GP VII, 322).

We are left with matter as such. Leibniz has two possible solutions. Thomas Aquinas and Duns Scotus regard matter as *quantitas continua*, as a real accident. Descartes regards matter as *res extensa*, as a separate substance. Both views see matter as a separate entity with absolute reality, even though in different senses, one as substance, the other as a real accident with absolute reality. Leibniz rejects both views: matter, for him, has only a phenomenal character. This means, if we include the phenomenality of relation which we shall discuss in the next section, that all physical concepts deal only with phenomena. However, at the end of the chapter, we shall endeavour to show that a feature arises in the concept of living energy which goes beyond this extreme phenomenalism.

Leibniz now considers secondary qualities, primary qualities, and matter (which the scholastics generally regard as a quality) purely as phenomena. There are no more qualities at all which could be made into separate entities with absolute reality by means of a *distinctio realis*. We can therefore say that in a certain manner the concept of quality has lost its independent meaning, though this does not mean that Leibniz dispenses with the term quality. For example in § 8 of the *Monadology* he talks of the qualities of monads:

'It is necessary that monads should have certain qualities, otherwise they would not even be beings ... and monads being without qualities would be indistinguishable the one from the other.'

However, the concept 'quality' has here lost its old ontological burden. The qualities by which the monads are distinguished from one another are their acts of perception (*perceptio*) and their acts of will (*appetitus*). Now, it is possible to term *perceptio* and *appetitus* qualities, but they are not qualities in the usual sense, they are not accidents, which would be distinguished from their substances as separate realities. As far as I know, no one has yet termed perception and appetition separate entities in this sense, and Leibniz certainly did not do this.

I must point out that on two occasions in the *Theodicy* Leibniz maintains that qualities are accidents which are distinguished from their substance by a *distinctio realis*.

'This shews that there is a real distinction between substance and its modification or accident, in spite of what some modern philosophers say, particularly the late Duke of Buckingham, who spoke of this in a little discourse on religion which has recently been reprinted' (§ 32).

The same view is repeated in § 87 in the *Theodicy*. In fact Buckingham had said in a very minor occasional work of 1685, *Short Discourse upon the Reasonableness of Man's having a Religion or Worship of God*: 'Accident, then, does not signify Being distinct from Body or Matter.' I cannot imagine why Leibniz should have mentioned this minor work, which in any case only treats the matter in passing. If we examine these passages from the *Theodicy* in their context then we see—at least this is the conclusion which I have reached—that Leibniz does not wish to return to the view of Duns Scotus. He is really more concerned with a defence against an extreme Spinozism which attempts to deny completely a real distinction between God and created substances.

In any case there are important passages where Leibniz completely rejects the idea of a real distinction between substance and accident, for example, in a letter to Malebranche (GP I, 321), and he also rejects the concept in the *Nouveaux Essais*. Finally there is a discussion of the whole matter in the correspondence with Des Bosses:

'Let us now look at real accidents which belong to this unitary thing as subject. You will agree, I think, that some of them are nothing but its modifications, which disappear accordingly when the thing itself disappears. However, it is asked whether there are not certain accidents which are more than modifications, but these seem completely unnecessary and whatever belongs to them and is beyond the modifications seems to belong to the substantial thing itself' (GP II, 458).

Des Bosses' answers do not seem to have been preserved in their entirety, at least they have not yet been published. It seems as though Des Bosses argued against Leibniz in support of the *distinctio realis*, which was only to be expected. Leibniz replies:

'You say that you cannot see that it should be impossible for anything to be real which is not substantial.'

He rejects this politely but unambiguously:

'Hence, I do not know whether there is a predicamental accident really distinguished from the subject which is not a predicable accident: and whether there is a predicable accident which is not a modification; just as I now doubt whether there is a predicamental accident distinguished from the subject which is not a modification' (GP II, 504).

I therefore think that Leibniz's opinion can be summarised as follows: neither secondary nor primary qualities nor matter are really distinct accidents with absolute reality which exist as separate entities side by side with substances, that is, for Leibniz, side by side with monads. Only monads have an absolute reality; secondary qualities, primary qualities, and matter have nothing but a phenomenal being.

§ 30. RELATIO

Leibniz always believed that relations were produced by thought and in the second book of the *Nouveaux Essais* he says:

'The division of the objects of our thoughts into modes, substances, and relations is sufficient for me. I think that qualities are only the modifications of substances and understanding adds relations to this' (GP V, 132).

There has been much discussion of the problem of the reality of relation partly because of the far-reaching meaning of the term. In the Middle Ages, relation was decisive for fundamental theological problems; today relation proves to be the fundamental category of mathematics and physics. The interpretation of relation as an accident with absolute reality, that is, as an entity, brings out the ontological problems particularly clearly, as such an interpretation of relation is much more problematical than it is in the case of quality.

If there is any category to which we wish to give the ontological status of mere representations, then relation offers the most obvious and convincing phenomena. At least certain relations depend upon mere notions, or are mere notions; no one has ever doubted this. Two obvious examples are right and left, which depend on the standpoint of the observer. Many relations of sequence and order depend upon quite arbitrary and transitory fixations. In children's games 'turns' are decided by counting rhymes. Leibniz points to precedence which forms a system of relations among human beings apparently dependent on arbitrary conventions.

'A moral legal situation serves, among other things, as the basis of a relation; as for example in the relation of an army commander or citizen. These relations are arbitrary or conventional as they depend upon agreements which people have made among themselves' (GP V, 231).

Every one who has attempted to determine the reality of relations has agreed that there are certain relations which have been arbitrarily determined by human thought. This sort of relation is called an *ens rationis*. Kant uses the term thought-thing (*Gedank-*

ending). Leibniz usually uses the simple translation 'being of reason' (*être de raison*).

'Relations and orders have something of the being of reason' (GP V, 210).

If we agree, in this way, that there are, at least, certain relations which are produced by thought, we must then ask whether there are also other relations with another kind of being. If we call the relations which arise from thought rational relations, and then distinguish these from real relations, we must ask what is the source of the reality of these other relations.

Duns Scotus gives us the first explicit answer, if I understand him correctly. From the ontological point of view Duns Scotus distinguishes three different relations: *relatio rationis*, *relatio formalis*, *relatio realis*. The *relatio rationis* is dependent upon what is determined by thought and is thus the relation which derives from thought. The *relatio formalis* embraces in essence the transcendental relations. The relations between transcendentals belong to the *relatio formalis* as do relations between the *esse bonum* and the *esse unum* of a substance and also the relation between the *esse bonum* and the substance itself. Duns Scotus also includes under this heading certain general relations whose interpretations have always caused difficulty, particularly difference. There are also a number of relations which are discussed in theology, for example the *esse creatum* of creatures (*Rep. Par.* II, I, 6). There are also real relations. These real relations are accidents in the strict meaning of the term, that is, independent entities which are differentiated from one another, from other accidents, for example qualities, and from the substratum which bears them, a substance or an accident, by a *distinctio realis*. In Ockham's words, this sort of relation is a *res absoluta realiter distincta*. Duns Scotus mentions as examples similarity and the father-son relationship, old examples of which Aristotle had given for this relation (*Op. ox.* II, 1, 4).

Ockham and the philosophers who followed attacked this idea of the real relation as being a *res absoluta realiter distincta*. Suarez, the English empiricists, Hobbes and Locke especially, and finally Leibniz himself, all oppose this view. All these philosophers believe that there is a distinction between a *relatio rationis* and a *relatio realis*; at least this is true of the English empiricists and, as we shall see, of Leibniz too. The question is whether the real relation can be understood as a *res absoluta realiter distincta* in the sense of Scotus, and if it cannot, how can it be understood? In my view Leibniz must be understood within the framework of this tradition. Bertrand Russell does not do this and frequently misunderstands Leibniz on relations.

The concept of relation as an absolute reality leads to an ontological multiplication *ad infinitum* as Ockham and others including Leibniz have shown, and is then irreconcilable with the concept of the accident as such.

The first problem is that of ontological multiplicity. This becomes particularly clear if we regard difference as an accident in the strict sense, which neither Thomas nor Duns Scotus does. According to this view, there would be a real difference between every substance, substance A would have a real accident 'difference from B' and naturally a real accident 'difference from C', etc. It is true that in the scholastic philosophy of the Middle Ages the number of substances was regarded as finite and so substance A would have had a finite number of accidents in 'differences from B, C . . .', but the number was very large and in addition was always in a state of constant mutation. Every time a new substance N appears there is a new accident in A 'difference from N' and every time a substance N passes away so the real accident in substance A, 'difference from N' also disappears. Furthermore, the interpretation of difference as a *res absoluta realiter distincta* also leads to an infinite regression. Substance A must be different from its accident 'difference from substance B'. This difference, for its part, must be a real accident and so substance A not only has to have a real accident 'difference from substance B', but also a real accident 'difference from the difference from B'. It is easy to recognise the infinite regress. The principle 'Entities should not be multiplied beyond necessity' could be particularly well applied against such an accumulation of beings in each individual thing.

Now, these remarks are not applicable to Duns Scotus, since he, subtle thinker that he was, perhaps because of these very ideas, did not regard difference as a *relatio realis* but as a *relatio formalis*. Difference is then not a *res absoluta* and the infinite regress cannot get going. Scotus regards sameness, on the other hand, as a real relation but here again he avoids the infinite regress because he regards the relation between an accident and the substance which bears it, in our case, the relation between sameness as a real accident and the substance which bears it, not as a real relation but only as a formal one. On the other hand the infinite regress seems unavoidable in the case of numbers. The scholastics included number under *quantitas discreta*, and the difficulties which arise from numbers were therefore discussed by Scotus, Ockham and Suarez under the heading of quantity. We include them here because, as we saw in Chapter IV, Leibniz subsumed quantity under relation and established the relative character of number. 'Numbers, unities, fractions have the nature of relations' (GP II, 304). Irrespective of how we decide the problem in categorial analysis we encounter ontological difficulties which come down to the fact that numbers can be counted. If the twoness of two substances A and B is an accident in the sense of a *res absoluta realiter distincta*, then a third entity exists side by side with the two entities, A and B, which have been counted. This third entity is the entity two, and not two as a general concept but as the twoness of the two substances. According to the ontological assumption, this two is also a *res absoluta*. There are, then, three entities, but this three is also an absolute entity, and so there are four entities and so on *ad infinitum*. The concept of the two as an absolute reality leads then to an infinite regress and consequently to a multiplication of being *ad infinitum*. Perhaps this is the reason why Duns Scotus hesitates to regard number as an absolute reality and, if this is the case, it would be sufficient cause for giving him the honorary title of *doctor subtilis*. Ockham saw this infinite regress and rejected it.

'Let us suppose a twoness. This twoness is a separate *res realiter distincta* from two unities through its being supposed. Hence, there are here three *res realiter distinctae*, namely two unities and one twoness, but there cannot be three things without threeness therefore there is a threeness distinct from the three unities which it is composed and in consequence there are four and so a fourness and hence a fiveness and so on *ad infinitum*' (In I. sent. D. 24q. 2P).

Leibniz points to this infinite regress as early as 1670.

'For real things are concrete, abstracts are not things, but modes of things and many modes are nothing but the relations of the thing to the understanding or the faculties of appearance. And indeed there is an infinite repetition of modes, and qualities of qualities and numbers of numbers which, if all these are things, gives rise not only to infinity but to contradiction' (*De stylo Nizolii* GP IV, 147).

Leibniz regards it as contradictory that we have to look upon entity as an *ens* and reality as a *res*, thus arriving at concepts which contain themselves:

'For if being is an *ens* and reality a *res*, if something is that something the same thing will be its own form or part of its own concept.'

We can ignore the question as to whether Leibniz was in a position to propound explicitly the contradiction which he maintains here and which does in fact exist. The resulting infinite accretion of beings was clearly seen by him. His opposition to the hypostasis of abstract concepts and his fundamental view that reality only exists in the concrete is clearly stated in paragraph XVII of the *Dissertatio de stylo Nizolii*. Perhaps it is no coincidence that Leibniz mentions Hobbes in the same paragraph shortly after the passages quoted above.

The fact that we have referred to Ockham on this question of the infinite accretion of beings in respect of numbers does not mean that there is any historical connection between Leibniz and Ockham. I look upon the connection, as always in this work, merely from the point of view of the history of ideas. As far as I can see, Leibniz never specifically refers to Ockham. On the other hand, I would hesitate to ascribe the discovery of the difficulties mentioned in the *Dissertatio* to Leibniz. I would rather assume that there is a dependence here which came down to him through his teachers, Thomasius or Scherzer. In any case, the literature which the young genius quotes in his early works contains ample references which could have acted as a stimulus.

The second difficulty arises from specific determinations which belong to the accident as such. If we accept the Aristotelian presupposition that only individuals are real—Leibniz agrees completely with this point of view—then it follows that every accident must be founded upon an individual being, a substance. This is certainly a very plausible demand. Consider bravery, for example; according to Aristotle this can only exist as a generality if it is found in concrete characteristics of this and that brave man. Any instance of being brave is also a property, which is an accident and must therefore be based upon a concrete individual. Only a single individual human being or perhaps an individual animal can be brave, certainly only an individual living creature. Thomas Aquinas, in his commentary on Aristotle's *Metaphysics*, formulates this Aristotelian theory in the words: '*esse accidentis est inesse.*' This In-being means 'to be in an individual single being'. As we can clearly see from the example of bravery, this makes difficulties for the theory of relations. Though a relation generally exists between two objects, there are also, of course, numerous relations between more than two objects and Leibniz paid attention to them. Conversely, identity, regarded as the relationship of an object with itself, has always been the cause of great difficulties. Let us consider first the most frequent form of relation that exists between two objects. The obvious example is the two, the two regarded as the concrete twoness of two objects. If we interpret it as an accident in the sense of *res absoluta realiter distincta*, then we immediately come up against difficulties. This two is certainly not an individual being and must therefore be inherent in an individual being as an accident. The question is, in which? The difficulties which arise here were seen early on and they play a leading part in the dispute between Ockham and Duns Scotus over the reality of real relations. A relation, considered as a real accident, would be an accident which stood so to speak with one foot in one substance and the other in another, and this contradicts the idea of an accident as inherent in a particular individual being. In any case, such a view would not solve the problem but would merely postpone it as we saw in the case of the two. The function of the two is to unite two individual objects; if we regard it as an individual object we have not solved the problem but merely put it off.

This problem arises in the discussion between Leibniz and Newton on absolute space.

We have already pointed out that the correspondence between Leibniz and Clarke is really a correspondence between Leibniz and Newton and that Leibniz himself prepared the correspondence for the press. Newton demands absolute space and Leibniz opposes it. We must, of course, ask ourselves what we mean by absolute space and Newton expresses himself very tortuously on this question. Leibniz interprets the Newtonian view of absolute space in the terms of a *res absoluta* and there then remains only the three ancient possibilities. Space is a substance (a point of view which Leibniz held during his atomic period), or space is a quality with absolute reality, or space is a relation with absolute reality. Until we have a more exact exposition of Newton's ontological assumptions we cannot be sure whether such a view does justice to him.

As Leibniz's categorial analysis deems space to be a system of relations there is an interesting discussion on the reality of a relation in this correspondence and there is no better way of expressing the fundamental problem than to use Leibniz's own words in his fifth letter (§ 47):

'I shall allege another example, to show how the mind uses, upon occasion of accidents which are in subjects, to fancy to itself something answerable to those accidents, out of the subjects. The ratio or proportion between two lines L and M, may be conceived three several ways; as a ratio of the greater L to the lesser M; as the ratio of the lesser M to the greater L; and lastly, as something abstracted from both, that is, as the ratio between L and M without considering which is the antecedent and which the consequent; which the subject and which the object. And thus it is, that proportions are considered in music. In the first way of considering them, L the greater; in the second, M the lesser, is the subject of that accident, which philosophers call relation. But which of them will be the subject in the third way of considering them? It cannot be said that both of them, L and M together, are the subject of such an accident; for if so, we should have an accident in two subjects, with one leg in one, and other in the other, which is contrary to the notion of accidents. Therefore we must say, that this relation, in this third way of considering it, is indeed out of the subjects; but being neither a substance, nor an accident, it must be a mere ideal thing, the consideration of which is nevertheless useful.'[43]

I think that Russell has misunderstood the sense of this passage in his book on Leibniz. Perhaps he did not consider sufficiently the historical precedents which come to light here. Furthermore, Russell was at that time so deeply involved in his dispute with Bradley that he was opposed to the least trace of idealism, and there is a good deal of idealism in Leibniz's ontological interpretation of space. Objectively Russell might well have had a good deal of sympathy for Leibniz's interpretations of space.

It might well be that for Russell the third case was the true interpretation of the relation. In the example which Leibniz gives, a relation is certainly not a property of L or of M, but rather, if it is twofold, a relation between two elements. Leibniz's additional example cannot perhaps be bettered. The octave is not a property of the lowest note or of the highest note, but the harmony of two tones. Russell is one of those who has done much to clear up this question. A twofold relation is a statement about two elements. This is clearly seen in the equation $a = b$, which is a simultaneous statement about a and b and in many problems it is advantageous to write it in the following way: $= (a, b)$.

If we keep this in mind, the ontological consequences soon become clear. A relation cannot be an accident in the sense of a *res absoluta*, a relation cannot be an independent entity. There is certainly an echo of Ockham's point of view in Leibniz's attitude. Leibniz says that the hypostasis of the relation is an example of a habit of mind, and he means when he says this a bad habit of mind, which leads us to add something to certain properties. Leibniz thus opposes our intellectual bad habit of thinking up extra things which do not exist and Russell is certainly in full agreement with this.

The traditional argument that an accident with absolute reality would be an accident with one foot in one substance and the other in another, clarifies the problem in the most instructive possible way. This argument is repeated by Leibniz on a number of occasions.

Relation is not, therefore, an absolute reality in things themselves, but rather a determination which thought brings to things. We may then quote in conclusion what Leibniz says in the *Nouveaux Essais*: '. . . and to this the understanding adds relations'.

This would be an extreme form of nominalism and certainly opposed to Leibniz's ideas if the understanding which produces relations were not also the divine understanding. Thus, Leibniz can say:

'However, although relations spring from the understanding, they are not void of foundation and reality. For the first understanding is the origin of things' (GP V, 132).

§ 31. ENS RATIONIS, ENS MENTALE, PHAENOMENON

Up to now our chief concern has been Leibniz's polemics. We have seen that he was opposed to the view of qualities and relations as accidents with absolute reality and that he was also opposed to the view that qualities and relations were separate entities. If we then ask what was his own positive metaphysics, we find the same gap that he complained about in other people. Leibniz is too rarely clear and definite, is too often obscure and inexact. We must try to clarify things as far as possible.

We can formulate the views which we have discussed in the two preceding sections as a proposition in categorial analysis by saying that not only quantity but also quality is included in relation. Leibniz only admits monads and their relations. Leibniz's positive contribution to ontology concentrates on determining the being of relation. There are essentially three concepts which we shall now discuss: *ens rationis*, *ens mentale*, *phaenomenon*.

The old ontological term *ens rationis* suggests itself for the ontological characterisation of the relations contributed by understanding. *Ens rationis—ens reale* have always designated the immediately apparent contrast between that which is thought and that which actually exists. However, the problem of transcendentals intrudes into this dual terminology and Duns Scotus sees the necessity for three terms: *ens rationis*, *ens formale*, and *ens reale*. This tripartite division is not to be found prior to Duns Scotus, and certainly not in the work of Thomas Aquinas. Subsequently it is only retained in the Scotist school of philosophers. Ockham and Suarez do not adopt it but keep to the old duality of *ens rationis* and *ens reale* in spite of the fact that their position is not far removed from that of Scotus. In Suarez *ens rationis* is a technical term. Kant uses the term *ens rationis* in the table of the concept of nothing for an empty concept without an object and calls it a thought-thing (*Gedankending*).

'Or like certain new fundamental forces which, though entertained in thought without self-contradiction, are yet also in our thinking unsupported by any example from experience, and are therefore not to be counted as possible' (A291 B347).

The old example of an *ens rationis* is a mythical beast such as a unicorn.

It can readily be seen that, because of the new concept of possibility, this meaning of *ens rationis* is of no use to Leibniz. According to Leibniz's definition of possibility anything which is free from contradiction is also possible. If we take the old example of the unicorn, then the concept of such an animal is free from contradiction, and it is possible. Perhaps it does not exist in the actual world, because not all possibilities can be present in one single world, but among the possible worlds there is one, at least, but perhaps many, perhaps infinitely many worlds in which there are unicorns. If, on the other hand, the concept of the unicorn contains a contradiction, then it is not a concept at all, and so it cannot appropriately be termed an *ens rationis*.

Under these circumstances we find a whole series of passages in which Leibniz terms thought which is free from contradiction, and particularly relation, an *ens rationis* (GP V, 210).

However, if I understand his use of the term correctly, he prefers to use *ens rationis* for those things which in his view are not even possible and particularly for the non-existent entities of the extreme scholastics. In an appendix to the *Theodicy*, he terms a force which chooses, without having a reason for making a specific choice, an *ens rationis*. Such a faculty cannot exist in the actual or any possible world as it would conflict with the principle of sufficient reason. These philosophers are merely using empty words to which nothing corresponds. Leibniz can then say:

'It is also true, fortunately, that it does not exist anywhere, and that it is a being of rational reason, as some scholasts call the fictions which are not even possible. For my part, I would prefer to call them beings of non-rational reasoning' (GP VI, 432).

The purely negative meaning of *ens rationis* in this passage is apparent.

Generally speaking, Leibniz uses the term *ens mentale* on the rare occasions when he is being careful about his terminology. Thus he writes in letters to Des Bosses:

'But the common relation of each of two things is merely a mental thing (*ens mentale*), whose basis is the modifications of the individual things' (GP II, 486).

'For, in fact, it cannot be denied that the natures of all possible single numbers are furnished, at least in the divine understanding (*in divina mente*)' (GP II, 305).

However, there are other terms; in the *Nouveaux Essais* Leibniz again terms relation an *ens rationis*.

'Relations and orders have something of the being of reason, although they are based upon things' (GP V, 210).

There is also the term 'ideal thing' and in the fifth letter to Clarke Leibniz talks of space as a 'mere ideal thing'.

The proper expression for the being of relation is phenomenon, and it is also the one which has established itself historically, as in phenomenalism or the phenomenal character of nature governed by mathematical laws. Leibniz uses the term phenomenon (in the French texts *phénomène*) but he also uses the Latin term *apparentia* (French: *apparences*). We thus arrive at a simple plan of being. Monads are the only real things; everything else is phenomenon.

'You judge very well, Sir, that my monads are not atoms of matter, but simple substances, endowed with power (I would add of perception and appetition) of which bodies are merely phenomena' (to Bourget, GP III, 559).

'True substances are merely simple substances or what I call monads. And I believe that there are only monads in nature, the remainder being only the phenomena which result from them' (to Dangicourt, E 745*b*).

The best survey of the meaning of phenomenon is the paper, *De modo distinguendi phaenomena realia ab imaginariis*, which was first published by Erdmann. The title reveals that Leibniz feels the necessity for distinguishing several types of phenomena. The first meaning of phenomena is found in dreams and flights of imagination; Leibniz mentions the golden mountain and the centaur (GP VII, 319). Then, in accordance with tradition, he regards secondary qualities as phenomena, added to which is the specific view of Leibniz that all primary qualities including matter were phenomena. He summarises the whole by saying (in a quotation which we have already used):

'I can demonstrate that not only light, heat, colour and similar qualities in bodies are apparent, but also size, form and movement' (GP VII 322).

Leibniz finds himself in agreement with Plato on this question of the phenomenality of nature as a whole.

'It is demonstrable that all bodies are nothing but phenomena, this, in my opinion, is what Plato was well aware of' (to Foucher, GP I, 391).

It is even possible that the whole of life including all phenomena is merely a dream, and apparently this is what the Platonists wanted to say.

'What if our nature did not happen to be capable of real phenomena, surely we ought not to accuse God but rather thank Him for arranging that those phenomena, though they cannot be real are nevertheless in agreement, and showing us what for all the purposes of life are the equivalent of real phenomena. What, indeed, if this short life is nothing but a long sleep from which we awake in dying, which is what the Platonists seem to think?' (GP VII, 321).

Leibniz also says much the same in *Examen des principes du R. P. Malebranche*:

'Thus it seems that with philosophical rigour bodies do not deserve the name of substance; and this appears to have been the view of Plato, who remarked that they are only transitory beings, which do not exist for more than a moment' (GP VI, 586).

This is certainly a bold interpretation from our point of view, schooled as we are in the history of philosophy. Leibniz is only concerned with the thesis that bodies are phenomena and this is, in fact, a thesis which Plato propounded in the *Republic*, and which he indicated in *Phaedo*. Leibniz ignores the fact, however, that in Plato's work the opposite of phenomena is quite different from what it is for him. Plato contrasts phenomena with ideas, Leibniz with monads, in other words it is the general which we find in Plato and the individual in Leibniz. This fundamental difference in the opposite concept must naturally alter the concept of the phenomenon. It is true that we often find daring interpretations of this sort in Leibniz; when he draws on the history of philosophy he often finds that the thesis alone is sufficient for him. That the context in which the thesis occurs gives it a quite different meaning he often ignores.

He thus arrives at what I consider to be a quite un-Platonic relationship between *ens mentale* and phenomenon. The most telling passage again occurs in the *Examen*:

'So, to put it in one word, a body has no real unity at all; it is only an aggregate, which the scholastics call a *per accidens*, an assembly like a troop; its unity comes from our perception. It is a being of reason or rather of the imagination, a phenomenon' (GP VI, 586).

Not only the secondary qualities but also all the primary ones are merely *in mente*. The totality of nature, in fact, only exists *in mente*. This is in sharp and conscious contradiction to Descartes. Leibniz sees nature as nothing but a complex of relations. If this were true for Descartes and if, in particular, the *res extensa* were for Descartes merely a complex of relations, then presumably nature would have lost its substantial character and would probably have been regarded by Descartes in much the same way as by Leibniz. Leibniz sees the ontological character of nature as *ens mentale* as an immediate consequence of having a system of relations. We must, however, remember that this *esse in mente* is first and foremost an *esse in mente divina* and that only secondarily and derivatively is it an *ens mentale* of our thought.

The connection with thought distinguishes Leibniz's theory from Plato's. Plato distinguishes between noumena and phenomena; if we wanted to say that one of the two is only thought, this could only be the ideas. The terms *noumena* and *noeta* show this quite clearly. The reversal is plain, when Leibniz describes space in its phenomenal being as a *chose idéale*, using the term which derives from *ideal* for the very thing which Plato does not regard as an idea but as a phenomenon.

He expounds the relation of phenomenon to thought in Chapter 12 of Book 11 of the *Nouveaux Essais*. Locke's opinions as presented in the *Essay on Human Understanding* are summarised as follows:

'Modes are either simple (like a dozen, or a score, which are made up of simple ideas of the same sort; that is unities) or mixed (like beauty) into which there enter simple ideas of different sorts.'

To this Leibniz replies:

'It may be that a dozen and a score are only relations and are only constituted by their relation to the understanding. The unities are separate and the understanding puts them together however diverse they may be. However, although relations are of the understanding they are not without foundation and reality. For the first understanding is the origin of things: and even the reality of all things, with the exception of simple substances, only consists in the foundation of the perception of phenomena of simple substances' (GP V, 132).

Leibniz is here emphasising the arbitrariness of such groupings. The understanding can put things together as it likes, however diverse they may be, and from this it follows that it is the understanding which does the putting together. This is a completely plausible and well-established argument, which clarifies the connection between numbers and the understanding which makes use of them in order to count.

The same train of thought occurs again at the end of the chapter. Locke's view is reported in such a way as to suggest that as well as the ideas of single substances, like the idea of a human being or of a sheep, there are also ideas of collective beings, the idea of an army of men, the idea of a herd of sheep. To this Leibniz replies that in his view such collective beings only exist in imagination.

'This unity of the idea of aggregates is very plausible, but at bottom it must be admitted that this unity of collections is only a relation founded in what is present in every one of the single substances separately. Thus, beings having their existence in aggregations have achieved no other unity but a mental one; and in consequence their entity is also mental, in a certain fashion, or phenomenal like that of the rainbow' (GP V, 133).

§ 32. THE TWOFOLD PLAN OF BEING IN THE THEORY OF TWO WORLDS

The strict division between the monads and their modifications (*perceptio* and *appetitus*) which exist *an sich* on the one hand, and relations which are merely phenomenal on the other, leads to a theory of two worlds.

This division into monads and phenomena is also a division according to the kinds of law obeyed. Monads, the thinking beings, act according to moral laws; bodies act, of necessity, according to mechanistic laws. This is in effect the old division of man into soul and body. Leibniz says in § 78 of the *Monadology*:

'These principles have given me a way of explaining naturally the union or, rather, mutual agreement of the soul and the organic body. The soul follows its own laws, and the body likewise follows its own laws; and they agree with each other by virtue of the pre-established harmony between all substances since they are all representations of one and the same universe.'

In the *Considérations sur les principes de vie* which appeared in the *Histoire des Ouvrages des Savans* in 1705 Leibniz says:

'Souls follow their laws which consist in a certain development of perceptions according to good and evil: and bodies follow their laws which consist of the laws of motion; nevertheless, these two beings which are of a completely different genre agree together' (GP VI, 540).

This is the doctrine of the two realms and the pre-established harmony between them which plays an important part in the *Monadology*. For example, Leibniz says (§ 79):

'Souls act according to the laws of final causes through appetitions, ends and means. Bodies act according to the laws of efficient causes or motions. And the two realms, that of efficient causes and that of final causes, are in harmony with one another.'

Leibniz also mentions the two realms in the *Theodicy* § 339 and § 118. In Gottsched's translation, Richter, the first translator, defines the difference in the following terms:

'By the realm of Grace the author understands the realm of spirits or of reasonable creatures and by the realm of Nature the realm of irrational and physical creatures.'

This statement could hardly be correct, if we are to understand by it that the souls of men belong to the realm of grace and animals belong to the realm of nature. In my view all monads belong to the realm of grace, whether as human beings they have the power of *apperceptio* or as animals and other lower monads only the power of *perceptio*. To the realm of nature belong the bodies of all monads with their phenomenal being. As Leibniz said in the passage which we quoted above, we are concerned with two different types of being. We are concerned, then, with two realms, which are completely different in their being and in the laws which are valid in them. In the physical realm of nature we can only speak of the mechanical categories, there is only matter, movement, form and size. They are phenomena and are strictly and exclusively determined by purely mechanical laws. In the moral realm of grace there are souls with their acts of will and imagination and in this realm everything goes according to the laws of final causes. Both worlds are joined like two clocks which keep the same time by the law of pre-established harmony. Thus the course of perceptions and the course of mechanical happenings are of themselves independent, but pre-established harmony brings about an exact correspondence between the two. In this way Leibniz achieves a solution of the body–soul problem, as he suggested in § 78 of the *Monadology*. It cannot be denied, however, that Leibniz's solution is a highly artificial one and has consistently given offence because of this artificiality.

Leibniz also arrives at a solution to the problem of freedom by his doctrine of the two realms. For the Greeks and for the medieval philosophers the problem of freedom was not an urgent one. The general attitude, as represented by Aristotle, was that only the movements of the constellations were subject to fixed laws. On earth many things happen by sheer chance. For this school of thought an eclipse of the sun or the moon is subject to fixed laws, but the weather is subject only to chance. Since very little on earth is subject to the laws of nature there is plenty of scope for the free action of human beings. That a human being can do or not do what he ought is not a problem according to this view of the laws of nature. It only starts to become a problem when the regularity of nature is regarded as universal. This was considered by Greek atomists, but the problem only becomes urgent when nature is regarded as a complete and unimpugnable complex of laws. We are told that Newton discovered the laws of gravity when he saw an apple fall from a tree. This is a good story and an excellent illustration of Newton's discovery. Newtonian physics means that the laws of nature are not only valid for the sky, but that they have the same validity on earth, in other words, that they govern the whole of nature without exception. There is then the urgent problem of how, in a scheme of nature which is so bound by laws, it is possible for man to exert his free will. Leibniz justifiably claims that his doctrine of the two realms, taken in conjunction with the doctrine of pre-established harmony, offers a solution to the problem of freedom. We may object that the artificiality of the doctrine of the pre-established harmony also makes this a highly artificial solution to the problem of freedom. Even so, we have to concede that by his solution Leibniz clarified the problem.

Kurt Hildebrand's interpretation now becomes intelligible.[44] Hildebrand interprets Leibniz's work purely from the point of view of two worlds and brings him into a close relationship with Plato whom he interprets in the same way. There can be no doubt that there is good ground in both Leibniz's work and in

Plato's for such an appraisal, as is shown by the passages quoted by Hildebrand and the considerations which we have put forward. However, I should maintain primarily on systematic grounds that the theory of two worlds does not represent the last word either for Plato or for Leibniz.

§ 33. ENS FICTITIUM

A whole series of physical and mathematical problems force Leibniz to modify this basically very compact theory of the twofold plan of being. I should like to remind the reader once more that the conclusions which we offer here are meant in a purely systematic sense and that we are still not in a position to gain an adequate overall view of the historical sequence in Leibniz's own development, as not all the material is yet available.

Leibniz is forced by the problems of complex or imaginary numbers and of the differential to introduce the concept of the *ens fictitium*. One cannot tell how this concept fits into Leibniz's system as a whole, but it certainly does not fit into a twofold scheme of being.

Imaginary numbers had been discovered in Leibniz's day, and Leibniz himself played an active part in these discoveries. At first sight an imaginary number, the square root of a negative number, seems to be a paradox. Then it was seen that at least in some ways it was possible to operate with imaginary numbers (GP II, 305). There are expressions containing imaginary numbers which are constructed in such a way that the imaginary numbers disappear when certain operations are carried out. Expressions of this sort formed with imaginary numbers do not by any means always lead to contradictions, but at least in some cases to normal results. Thus, it was seen that imaginary numbers could be used as the roots of equations. It can then easily be seen that the general rule that an equation has as many roots as its degree indicates can only be generally valid if we include the imaginary roots. It is easy to construct equations of the third degree, which have one real and two imaginary or complex roots, and Leibniz did this (GP I, 340).

Leibniz drew the inference that complex numbers were a

justifiable and logical concept in mathematics and went on to draw the equally justified inference that the concept of a complex number does not contain a contradiction (GP II, 305; GM III, 524).

However, if we consider his scheme of being *in toto* we find that a difficulty arises at this point. All concepts which are free from contradiction exist, and for Leibniz this means that they exist in divine thought; they exist therefore in a possible world (GM III, 551).

It may be that in a possible world certain realities correspond to them, it may also be that only relationships between realities correspond to them. Thus for example every natural number, no matter how large, is realised in some possible world, and indeed in the real world because of its infinite nature. As there is an infinite number of monads in the real world, there is for every natural number, N, a number of monads which corresponds exactly to the number expressed by N, but Leibniz saw no way of realising an imaginary number in the actual world or in any of his possible worlds. There was, therefore, no other way open to him but to accept and use the concept *ens fictitium* for the purposes of this problem.

Later Gauss took this idea as his starting point. The proof of the existence of complex numbers presupposes the notion that complex numbers can be shown to designate either actual objects or the relations between actual objects. Gauss's exposition of complex numbers represents the successful accomplishment of this idea (*Works*, II, 175 f.). Whether there is a connection here between Guass and Leibniz I am unable to say. As far as Leibniz is concerned complex numbers when interpreted in Gaussian terms would represent relations between possible objects and would therefore be justified in a Leibnizian sense.

Leibniz also makes use of the term *ens fictitium* when interpreting the differential calculus. Whether he invented the term for use in the differential calculus or with imaginary numbers can only be finally determined when all the manuscript material is available. In his letter to Des Bosses of 3 March 1706 he writes:

'I consider, philosophically speaking, infinitely small sizes no more than infinitely great or no more infinitesimal than infinituple. For, in brief,

I consider both of them fictions of the mind, useful for calculation, of the same order as imaginary roots in algebra. Meanwhile, I have shown that these expressions are of great use for the abbreviation of thought and thus for invention, and that they cannot lead to error, since it is sufficient to substitute for the infinitely small as small a thing as one may wish, so that the error may be less than any given amount, hence it follows that there can be no error. R. P. Gouye who objected to this, does not seem to have understood me properly' (GP II, 305).

What has just been said of imaginary numbers also holds good for differentials. Leibniz was right in assuming that the differential calculus was free from contradiction and also that the differential was a concept which was free from contradiction. However, it must also exist as a concept which is free from contradiction in the sense that it is realised in one, at least, of the possible worlds.

This is the more difficult for Leibniz to interpret because he regards the differential quotient as a proper fraction between two differentials. He adds to this the products and powers of differentials, for example, $dy.dy$ and $(dx)^2$, as well as the iterated differences, ddx, $dddx$, etc., to use Leibniz's notation. All these isolated expressions cannot be realised in any world, and Leibniz's designation of them as *entia fictitia* while not solving the problem does at least name it.

Cassirer[45] sets great store by this interpretation of the differential as an *ens fictitium* and he regards it as an embodiment of Leibniz's conviction that not only the concepts of the differential but that all pure concepts arise from thought alone. It is possible that Cassirer is assimilating the new concepts of imaginary numbers and differentials too closely to the classical concepts. Natural numbers, themselves the prototype of the classical concept, also arise in Leibniz's view from thought alone, but they can justify themselves by being realised. This justification is, however, lacking in the case of imaginary numbers and differentials, so that when Cassirer, without further ado, classes these new concepts with the old mathematical concepts, instead of re-interpreting them, he is obscuring a difference which presented Leibniz with great difficulties, but which was, nevertheless, of great importance to him.

§ 34. ENS SEMIMENTALE

Even if we disregard the problem of the *ens fictitium* it is still impossible to subsume all being under a strict dichotomy: real being (*ens reale*) or mere appearance (phenomenon). Leibniz sees the necessity for another concept, which he calls by different names. From one point of view it is the *ens semimentale*, from another *semiens* or, in concrete cases, *semisubstantia* and *semiaccidens*, or from a third point of view it is termed the *phenomenon bene fundatum*. Although, fundamentally, we are concerned with a single concept, we shall endeavour to distinguish the terms: *ens semimentale* and *phaenomenon bene fundatum*. We find a combination of both terms in a letter to Des Bosses:

'We understand that such a matter, that is the principle of the phenomenon, persists and adheres to its entelechy, and thus a secondary matter results from several monads, with derivate powers, actions, phenomena which are not entia by aggregation and are thus *semimentalia* like the rainbow and other *phenomena bene fundata*' (GP II, 306).

In another letter to Des Bosses dated 19 August 1715, Leibniz uses the terms, *semiens*, *semisubstantia* and *semiaccidens*.

'I therefore prefer it to be said that not substances but appearances survive, that these are, however, not illusory, like sleep or like the sword pointed at us from a concave mirror or the cart full of hay which Dr. Faustus consumed but true phenomena, that is in the sense that the rainbow or the parhelion is an appearance: indeed as, according to the Cartesians, colours are appearances. And it can be said that compound entities, which are not one in themselves or are not contained in one spirit by a chain of substance are *semientia*; aggregates of simple substances, like an army, or a heap of stones are *semisubstantia*; colours, smells and tastes are *semiaccidentia*' (GP II, 504).

Leibniz appends to this letter the table which is reproduced in abbreviated form on facing page.

In order to understand how this concept is formed it is probably best to begin with Leibniz's own example of the rainbow. No one can see a rainbow without experiencing delight in it. It is an object in which human feeling for nature, the myth and the natural science of our own day all meet. The explanation of the rainbow

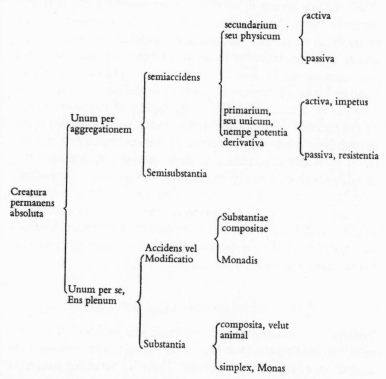

is an old theme in physics: given a certain configuration of observer, the rays of the sun and the wall of rain the rainbow must occur as a phenomenon of refraction.

But what is a rainbow? The child observes it, as he observes everything in the world, and runs towards it to catch hold of it, but we say to him, you cannot catch hold of it, for it is nothing. At least this is what we say if we have been educated in modern science, but if we are less well-informed we give the child one of the more ancient and more lovely explanations. Nevertheless we are still faced with the problem, what is a rainbow? Of course, it is not a body, it is not a thing, but on the other hand neither is it a dream, a mere phantasma. On the contrary it is the object of certain well-defined natural laws. Of course it is possible to dream of a rainbow just as it is possible if endowed with a lively visual gift to imagine a rainbow, but the actual rainbow which spreads across the sky after a shower of rain is something different. It is certainly only a phenomenon, but it is a well-established one. It is certainly an *ens mentale*, because it is dependent upon the human power of sight. In order to see a rainbow we must be in full possession of our faculties of vision, we may not even be colour-blind and thus the rainbow depends upon the faculty of sight, but only partly. It depends partly on the faculty of vision and partly on the rain and the sun, and for this reason, when Leibniz regards the rainbow from the standpoint of the spontaneity of the observer he is able to confine it to an *ens semimentale*, but he is able simultaneously to extend it to a *semiens*, a *phenomenon bene fundatum* if he looks at it from the point of view of the laws of nature.

It can perhaps be argued that to use the rainbow as an example in order to define the *semiens* is not entirely unexceptionable from the logical point of view, but metaphysics like many other sciences has to define by means of examples.

§ 35. PHAENOMENON BENE FUNDATUM

Perhaps the concept of the *phaenomenon bene fundatum* (the *phénomène bien fondé*) is the most important concept in the whole of the later stages of Leibniz's philosophy. There is a revealing passage in a letter to Remond de Montmort written on 10 January 1714 and published by Des Maizeaux in 1720. In this letter the sixty-eight-year-old Leibniz is surveying his life's work:

'It is true that I did not plumb the greatest depths until I had talked to M. Huygens in Paris. When I looked for the final causes of mechanics and of the laws of motion I was very surprised to see that it was impossible to find them in mathematics and I had to return to metaphysics. This is what caused me to turn back to entelechies and led me from the material to the formal and finally, after many false starts and corrections, made me understand that monads or simple substances are the only true substances and that material things are only phenomena, but well-founded and well bound up. Plato and even the later Academics and Sceptics managed to appreciate this partially, but these gentlemen who came after Plato did not make such good use of it as he' (GP III, 606).

Leibniz says much the same in his *Examen des principes du R. P. Malebranche* in 1711 (published by Des Maizeaux in 1720):

'There is even good reason to doubt whether God created anything but monads or substances without extent and whether bodies are anything but phenomena resulting from these substances. My friend whose opinions I have reported to you agrees that he also inclines towards this view, when he reduces everything to monads or simple substances and their modifications together with the phenomena which result from them, whose reality is demonstrated by their coherence, which distinguishes them from dreams' (GP VI, 590).

Phenomena, too, are thus endowed with reality, in that they are in a system of relations which is governed by laws and I should like to think that this is the sense in which Leibniz ascribes reality to bodies.

'In truth, we consider that bodies are things and that phenomena are real' (GP II, 492).

Two important lines of Leibniz's thought merge in this concept of the *phenomenon bene fundatum* which, in spite of everything, is now found to have a certain reality. One line is the idea to which he subscribes after his brief atomistic period. This is Plato's thesis that material bodies are not substances but merely phenomena, simply appearances. To this line of thought is added another which, after a lengthy consideration of the problem, comes to the conclusion that we must distinguish two forms of phenomenal being and that nature considered mechanistically and represented by natural laws belongs to a well-founded phenomenality which contains a certain degree of reality. This last is the view of Plato.

Leibniz reflected upon the two types of phenomena in a short paper entitled: *De modo distinguendi phenomena realia ab imaginariis.* Erdman who first published this paper is of the opinion that Leibniz had worked on it for a long time and that it could scarcely have been written before the end of the century. As the title states, Leibniz is here distinguishing between real and imaginary

M

phenomena. As examples of imaginary phenomena he quotes the centaur and the golden mountain.

Leibniz puts forward essentially three criteria for real phenomena: they must have powerful, well-determined properties which agree with each other, they must agree with other real phenomena, and finally, and this is the strongest criterion of the three, a real phenomenon must be capable of pre-determination.

'But the strongest indication of real phenomena which is alone sufficient, is the successful prediction of future phenomena from past or present ones. This prediction is based upon the reason or hypothesis which up to the moment has always followed or else upon usage which has been observed up to now' (GP VII, 320).

From this conclusion we can see that Leibniz regards secondary qualities (light, colour, heat, flavour and similar qualities) as real phenomena of this sort, and then also the primary qualities, in which connection he makes particular mention of movement, form and size.

Matter, which appears in this paper under its Cartesian definition of *extensio*, is also regarded as a *phaenomenon bene fundatum*. Mass is mentioned in a letter to Des Bosses: 'Mass is nothing but a phenomenon, like the rainbow' (GP II, 390).

A more precise formulation of Leibniz's view would be to say that the laws of nature constitute reality. The things to which these laws refer may, it is true, merely have a phenomenal character and Leibniz always maintained this point of view, but inasmuch as these phenomena are the object of the laws of nature they must also be possessed, in a certain way, of reality, since phenomena are themselves real. Leibniz admittedly speaks only of a connection but his suggestion that phenomena must be capable of predetermination shows clearly that he is referring to the laws of nature when he speaks of this connection. Lawfulness as such, especially the lawfulness of nature, and this is, in my opinion, the fundamental thought, vouches for reality, even if, because of the character common to all natural laws of being systems of relations, this can only be the reality of a *phaenomenon bene fundatum*.[46]

§ 36. THE CONTINUUM OF BEING

The doctrine of the *ens fictitium*, the differentiation between *ens mentale* and *ens semimentale* and the concurrent differentiation between *phenomenon imaginarium* and *phenomenon reale* now lead logically to a modification of the twofold plan of being. There are not only different types of substances, or monads, but also different types of phenomena which are differentiated according to their ontological content and have varying grades of reality.

If we now attempt to clarify this gradation of being, we find that the highest being is the divine being, or God and that God is the *ens realissimum*. Next in order are the created monads, which are differentiated, in their turn (as we have seen) according to their grades of reality, and which form a continuous series in respect of this gradation of reality. The monads are followed by their modifications, perceptions and appetitions, which are also graded as can most clearly be seen in the case of perceptions. Perceptions range from the secure knowledge of eternal truths to the vaguest sensual impressions, to whose obscurity and confusion there is no lower limit. In the realm of phenomena there is a distinction between real phenomena and those phenomena which are purely imaginary, between phenomena which are governed by the laws of nature and those which are the product of dreams or the imagination. Somewhere, right down at the bottom, is the *ens fictitium*, which is indispensible for the process of thought, but for which Leibniz could find no independent ontological content. In this endless series of ontological grades, it is the boundary between real being, the being of the monads and their modifications, and phenomenal being which is the really interesting one. In the light of the twofold theory of being this boundary is not only absolute, it is an unbridgeable gulf. We have already seen in Leibniz's work a whole series of statements which express the absolute character of this boundary. It is a particular problem of physics, the problem of energy, which compels Leibniz to modify the absolute nature of this distinction. To the best of my knowledge, it was Guéroult who in his excellent investigation published in 1934 (*Dynamique et métaphysique Leibniziennes*) first recognised the full significance of this question.

The problem of energy interested Leibniz greatly from the purely physical point of view. His interest centres upon that value whose measure is mv^2 in Leibnizian terms or $\frac{1}{2}mv^2$ in modern terms. This is the value which remains constant in mechanical processes and Leibniz was involved in an argument as to whether it was mv which remained constant, as Descartes had affirmed, or whether it was mv^2 which was the constant value. This dispute was the subject of Kant's dissertation, *Gedanken von der wahren Schätzung der lebendigen Kräfte und Beurteilung der Beweise, deren sich Herr von Leibniz und andere Mechaniker bedient haben* (*Thoughts on the true estimation of living forces and a critique of the proofs used by Herr von Leibniz and other mechanicists*).

Kant saw that there was no absolute solution to this problem. Under certain presuppositions mv remains constant but Leibniz's presuppositions are more generally valid.

Interesting as these purely physical questions are, the ontological problems of energy are very complicated, and particularly so from the standpoint of Leibniz's ontology.

The question of the reality of energy is first made complicated because as *vis activa* it has the closest connection with the fundamental features of monads. Leibniz calls the being of monads a *vis activa*. If, however, the reality of monads depends upon their *vis activa* and if something analogous is present in mechanics, must we not also ascribe reality in some sense to this living energy? There is also a second problem, the transferability of energy; in the case of qualities, which Leibniz regarded as not transferable from one substance to another, their non-transferability led him to deny their reality. It is therefore understandable that the transferability of energy caused him to regard it as a special sort of reality which can move from one place to another. I am particularly happy to find that these views which arise from ontological considerations should coincide with Guéroult's views which spring from the theory of science and from physics. Mahnke seems to have been the first to notice this: 'Leibniz says of the features of the phenomenal world which are dynamic and not purely mathematical that they are something "more real" than extension and movement . . . indeed energy is what is real in motion' (*Leibnizens Synthese*, p. 129).

When Leibniz tries to explain this reality of living force in ontological terms, his plan of being leaves him no option but to go back to the concept of the real accident. I therefore think that the passage from the *Theodicy* which we quoted above must be taken as meaning that Leibniz interprets energy as a real accident in the sense of a *distinctio realis*. The old *formae* re-appear in Leibniz's work not only as *formae substantiales* in the concept of the monad, but also the notorious *formae accidentales* in the concept of living energy. However, this interpretation of living energy is never carried through to a conclusion, it remains a marginal problem and basically represents nothing more than a trial interpretation.

The doctrine of grades of being agrees with what was said in Chapter VIII about the problem of good. Everything which exists has a different grade of being in respect of its *esse bonum*, a *gradus entitatis*. Thus for example our world which is the best of all possible worlds is distinguished from all other possible worlds by having the highest grade of being. The problems of reality have led us to the same conclusions.

From a historical point of view it is interesting to note that this is a development of an Aristotelian idea. It is alive in the work of Descartes, who attached importance to the concept of a greater or lesser degree of reality, particularly with reference to *realitas objectiva*. The idea of grades of being is indicated in Aristotle's work and his categories show a clear gradation of being. Substances have more reality than accidents and in the table of the four fundamental categories relation is less real than either quality or quantity. This was emphasised by Thomas Aquinas and I believe that in so doing he is expressing Aristotle's own view.

Leibniz here again has combined an Aristotelian and a Platonic viewpoint. The twofold plan of being which allows nothing but monads and their phenomena derives from Plato, the relaxation of the theory of the two worlds into a graded series of modes of being shows Aristotle's influence. Plato, however, only adheres to a strict theory of two worlds in the middle dialogues. Nobody has tried harder than he did in the later dialogues to go beyond the idea of two worlds.

§ 37. NUMBER, SPACE, TIME, NATURE

A re-consideration of Leibniz's ontological interpretation of the fundamental concepts of the mathematical sciences will help us to summarise our ideas. We may best begin with a refutation of Bertrand Russell using Mahnke's summary. Mahnke says of Bertrand Russell:

'He, too, stands for (like Moore) a Platonic idealism or more exactly, if we are to exclude Natorp's interpretation of Platonic ideas as a function of knowledge, a realism of ideas, which instead of deriving general concepts from individual observations (*universalia post rem*) operates in the reverse way and finds spiritual and physical reality in a hypostatic world of ideas which is quite independent of objective realisation and spiritual actualisation (*universalia ante rem*). Russell criticises Leibniz only with regard to the hypostasis of the concept of subjects, regarding them as self-sufficient substances immanently bearing all synthetic relations as predicative attributes, which are, curiously enough, in pre-established harmony with one another. Russell for his part tries to derive substances and their attributes from the independent reality of relations since, according to his synthetic logic, subject-predicate judgements are merely special cases of more fundamental relational judgements' (p. 30 f.).

Even if Russell is very reluctant to express general ontological views, we must admit that Mahnke's summary accurately represents Russell's position at the time of his book on Leibniz. It demonstrates once more how much the personal standpoint of the author, in this case Russell, enters into any historical exposition.

We can see then that Leibniz's and Russell's ontological points are diametrically opposed to each other. Russell regards relations as the true reality and things, especially individual livings beings, more or less as mere modes of relational connections. Leibniz, on the other hand, sees things as the only reality, and only individual living beings are things; relations are merely the connections which the understanding established between things.

Nevertheless, Leibniz and Russell show a great measure of agreement over the fundamental importance of relation. Numbers are relations, space is a complex of relations and nature too, when explained in mechanistic terms, is a complex of relations, which subsumes all other relations and complexes of relations, number, space, time, form, dimension, motion, matter, within itself. Because there is a system of laws which underlie this system of relations we call this Newtonian nature, and it was in this light that Kant stated that nature consists of nothing but relations.

The difference between Leibniz and Russell lies in their answers to the ontological question: what is real, individuals or relations? Russell was still a young man when he wrote his work on Leibniz and regarded his point of view as a secure one; when Leibniz's views oppose his then Leibniz is wrong. It may be true that Russell can bring to light a large number of difficulties in Leibniz, but the question still arises as to whether a calm investigation of Russell's position at that time would not also bring to light a large number of difficulties.

However that may be, Leibniz's fundamental approach is worthy of the utmost attention. To reduce it to its simplest terms we can say: the number of things is not itself another thing, the space occupied by things is not itself a spatial thing, the relation between things is not a new thing and nature which represents the totality of laws describing and determining the movements of natural things is not, of itself, a natural thing.

I should like to think that Leibniz's point of view can be supported both historically and theoretically. It is backed by a long tradition. Leibniz may have acquired his knowledge of it from his teachers and would in any case have seen it stated in Suarez's works in a clear and historically well-grounded form. It may have been from Suarez that Leibniz drew his conviction that he was in agreement with Ockham, Thomas Aquinas and Aristotle. Suarez calls this the fifth view to be developed on this problem and gives it his approval, mentioning supporting passages from Ockham,

Gregory of Rimini, Hervæus, Thomas Aquinas and Aristotle (*Disp. Met.* XLVII, 2, 11).

There are many theoretical considerations which support Leibniz's point of view and today we should regard those which are concerned with the analysis of meaning as being of great importance. I believe that Leibniz has shown very clearly how we are to understand the fundamental ontological concepts. The meaning of unity, reality and actuality may be had from self-experience. I experience myself as something real and in the last resort, therefore reality means being like me. The *Monadology* and Leibniz's philosophy in general are the logical development of this statement. On the other hand, it would probably not be easy to give the origin of the meaning which reality has for Russell.

In view of the clarity and consistency with which Leibniz works out his point of view, it is not surprising that he achieves some very instructive expressions of it and in one of his very early works published in 1770, the *De stylo philosophico Nizolii*, we encounter the elegant statement which we have already quoted on page 148.

From the fact that he expresses himself thus in such an early work we may assume that Leibniz found stimulus for his fundamental approach from his teachers.

In his later works we find this fundamental thought completely stated both implicitly and explicitly. I would particularly mention the dispute on the reality of time and place which takes up so large a part of the correspondence with Clarke. The most telling statement is probably in paragraph 47 of the fifth letter; his opinion is, perhaps, condensed into the sentence: 'I will give another example of the habit of the spirit of forming for itself on the occasion of accidents which are in subjects something which corresponds to them outside the subjects.' If we were to paraphrase this sentence we might say: 'I want to give another example of that habit of mind which sees properties which exist in things and which allows itself to be misled by this to think of new things, which ought to exist outside and by the side of original things.'

CHAPTER XI

ENS PERFECTISSIMUM

§ 38. THE EXISTENCE OF GOD

ARISTOTELIAN metaphysics has a double goal: it is the doctrine of the *ens qua ens* and it is at the same time the doctrine of the *ens perfectissimum*. This dual goal is readily understandable when viewed within the framework of Greek thought. As the doctrine of *ens qua ens*, metaphysics leads us to a *metaphysica generalis*, in a certain sense to a *metaphysica transcendentalis*. I am using the term *transcendentalis* in the Aristotelian-scholastic sense, although I believe that the Kantian use of the term also preserves a genuine link with the Aristotelian–scholastic sense. As the doctrine of *ens perfectissimum*, metaphysics leads to a *theologia naturalis*.

Leibniz retains this dual goal of metaphysics. Metaphysics and more generally speaking, philosophy in general, is always simultaneously *theologia naturalis* for Leibniz. Studies on *theologia naturalis* are among his earliest works. His only major work, published as a sixty-year-old man, is the *Theodicy* and this is decidedly a work of natural theology. Nor can the problems of *theologia naturalis* be dismissed from his last works, the *Monadology*, and the correspondence with Clarke, and Leibniz can maintain with justification in the *Considérations sur les principes de vie* that the system of pre-established harmony presents a proof of God which was unknown up to that time. We can further say that it was one of Leibniz's goals to transfer to theology the strictness of definition and proof which is possible in logic and mathematics.

One of his earliest writings is the *Confessio naturae contra atheistas* which appeared in 1668. Erdmann published for the first time a paper entitled *De vita beata* and puts it as an early work, probably correctly. These two works show the breadth of Leibniz's *theologia naturalis*. The first develops the outlines of Leibniz's specific proof of God, the second expounds the Cartesian proof of God, a subject to the analysis and criticism of which Leibniz devoted a great deal of energy throughout his life.

The *Confessio naturae contra atheistas* belongs to Leibniz's atomistic period. It develops a purely mechanistic explanation of nature and refers to Democritus, Epicurus, Robert Boyle, Galileo, Bacon, Descartes and Hobbes. It demands that all scientific concepts should refer only to the nature of the body and its primary qualities. The logical and ontological consequences of this point of view have occupied us upon several occasions already. Leibniz is convinced that the mechanistic point of view leads to things that cannot be explained purely mechanistically. Why atoms should have a certain shape, size, and movement cannot, for example, be explained on the basis of mechanistic concepts. Only an intelligent creator of the world can be the origin of such things. In this sense Leibniz can entitle this particular section: 'Why the reason of physical phenomena cannot be deduced without the incorporeal principle, that is God' (GP IV, 105).

We find a different process of thought in the *De vita beata*. This work clearly relies on Descartes, and Leibniz takes over completely the Cartesian criterion of truth, namely that of which we have a clear and distinct idea. He repeats the Cartesian proof of the existence of God as the *ens perfectissimum*, whose perfection would be incomplete if he did not exist (GP VII, 96).

In later analyses of this proof, Leibniz discovers a gap, and his investigations of this occupy him intensively for a long time. Leibniz sees that the proof is not complete. It would have to be proved that the concept of an *ens perfectissimum* is free from contradiction. If the concept contained a contradiction in itself as, for example, the concept of the *numerus maximus* contains one, then no proof could be based upon it, since in that case any proposition at all could be deduced from it. Leibniz is convinced that the concept of the *ens perfectissimum* is free from contradiction, otherwise he would not have made use of the concept himself, but in order to constitute a proof this freedom from contradiction must first be demonstrated. As long as this gap is not filled, the Cartesian proof of the existence of God must be regarded as incomplete. It is clear to Leibniz that we are here concerned with the ontological proof of the existence of God, in the form in which Anselm of Canterbury first formulated it, and Leibniz consequently mentions the fact that Thomas Aquinas also regarded the ontological proof of the existence of God as incomplete (GP IV, 424).

Leibniz devoted a great deal of time to this problem, for example, in the *Meditationes* of 1684, in the letter to Huygens of 3 October 1690 and in the letter to Oldenburg of 28 December 1675. Leibniz was probably aware that he had seen this gap correctly, but that he too had failed to fill it.

Leibniz's own proof of the existence of God begins with the concept of possibility and is summarised in § 7 of the *Theodicy*:

'God is the first reason of things . . . . this regard or relation of an existent substance to simple possibilities can be nothing other than the understanding which has ideas of them; while to fix upon one of them can be nothing other than the will which chooses. . . . Its understanding is the source of essences and its will is the origin of existences. There in a few words is the proof of one single God with his perfections and, through him, of the origin of things.'

The line of thought is that possible worlds are only worlds which are thought of and which exist only in thought. Something which is thought, however, cannot exist without the existence of a being who thinks these thoughts. The proof therefore depends upon the idea that possible worlds are worlds which exist in thought. The nub of the argument is expressed in the *Monadology* (§ 43):

'It is also true that in God is not only the source of existences but also of essences, in so far as they are real, of what is real in the possible. For the understanding of God is the region of eternal truths or of the ideas upon which they depend, and without Him none of the possibilities would be real and not only would nothing exist but nothing would even be possible.'

Without God as a thinking being there are no possible worlds; this notion emanates from Leibniz's specific view that possible worlds are worlds which have been thought of. If we accept this pre-supposition we must admit that a thinking being exists who thinks the totality of possible worlds and thus the existence of God can be proved if essences are interpreted as things which have been thought.

§ 39. THE ATTRIBUTES OF GOD

The question of the attributes of God is a theme of *theologia naturalis* which has been much discussed. It was a very important problem for mediaeval philosophy, but it is also significant and revealing for the philosophy of Leibniz. A very large number of considerations belong here and I shall only mention the following: the unity of God (*unitus Dei*), the omniscience, the wisdom and the justice of God.

Leibniz was convinced that we are not confined to a *theologia negativa* in our perception of the attributes of God, for this would involve us merely in denying of God all the known properties of creatures. In the *Theodicy* he says (§ 4):

'It is just the same with the concepts of the justice and goodness of God. From time to time, people speak of them as though they had neither concept nor explanation of them. If this were so, we should not have reason to ascribe these properties to Him nor could we praise Him on account of them.'

Gottsched gives an interpretation of this passage, which I consider a good one:

'There are, among us, people who under the pretence of wanting to raise God up above all creatures, speak of His properties as though they were different from ours not in degree but in essence. They are constantly saying that we do not know what God's wisdom, goodness, justice etc. are. We do not understand their rules and intentions, the way in which they function and so on. But this is only trying to plunge us into a state of complete carelessness and security, for if we do not and cannot know what all these perfections are in God, we must neither ascribe them to God nor speak of them. If, however, we can no longer speak of them, there is nothing we can say of God which will evoke a concept of Him. For this reason, God will be a *je ne sais quoi* to the worldly-wise of this sort, just as He is to the Sevaramds, who call Him an inscrutable, unfathomable, incomprehensible being.'

Gottsched's statement that God's properties are different from ours not in essence but in degree is very probably Leibniz's own view, for he believed in the possibility of a true knowledge of God. In the introduction to the *Theodicy*, he says:

'One cannot love God without knowing His perfections and this knowledge contains the principles of true piety. This knowledge of God is possible because the properties of God can be found within us, though not in such a perfect form.'

God's wisdom as well as his goodness and justice differ from our own only in that they are infinitely more perfect.

We have to take this as meaning that all properties, when they are attributes of God, represent a pure, unbounded, infinite reality. When they are the properties of created beings they are bounded and finite. Leibniz says in *Remarques sur le sentiment du R. P. Malebranche* (1708):

'Perhaps the intention of the author, in saying that we recognise the essences of things in the perfections of God and that it is universal reason which illuminates us, is to make us observe that the attributes of God form the basis of simple notions which we have of things. Being, force, knowledge, diffusion, duration, taken absolutely, are in Him and not in creatures, except to a limited extent'[39] (GP VI, 578).

Similarly Leibniz says in the *Monadology* (§ 49):

'But in God these attributes are absolutely infinite or perfect and in the created monads or entelechies . . . there are only imitations of these attributes, according to the degree of perfection of the monad.'

On this difficult question Leibniz's ideas seem to be intelligible. They may be attacked and they may be regarded as false but they are comprehensible. I find insurmountable difficulties however even in merely understanding Leibniz's thesis that the fundamental concepts defined in his logic coincide with the attributes of God. We discussed this idea in the first part of this book and it is too frequently repeated for us to neglect it. We can appreciate the point of view from which the thesis is developed. The fundamental concepts, like the attributes of God, represent pure positive realities, but how are we to combine the two points of view, the logical and the theological? Attributes of God are unity, wisdom, justice, but are all these to be regarded as fundamental concepts? Unity might be, but I know of no place where Leibniz definitely classifies unity as a fundamental concept and it is hard to see how he could substantiate such a suggestion. The concept of unity is at least a close neighbour of the fundamental concepts, but how can wisdom and justice be such? Besides this, two theses clash at this point. According to Leibniz fundamental concepts are unattainable for us, but he says that the attributes of God are attainable, at least in a limited form. There is indeed a relevant qualification in a letter to Des Bosses:

'Would that incomprehensibility were an attribute of God alone, but it is too true that there is no part of nature which can be understood perfectly by us and this proves the περιχώρησις of things' (GP II, 412).

But if we take Leibniz at his word here there would be no knowledge of nature or of God and Leibniz certainly had no wish to be as sceptical as that. We are left, then, with no choice but to doubt the alleged connection between the fundamental concepts and the attributes of God. Leibniz the great synthesiser probably allowed himself to be misled here by his enthusiasm for synthesis and saw a connection which could hardly exist in the form which he proposes.

CHAPTER XII

METAPHYSICS

§ 40. LEIBNIZ'S METAPHYSICAL OBJECTIVES AND METHODS

THE possibility of metaphysics has always been doubted and Leibniz is on the defensive. He begins his paper, *De primae philosophiae emendatione* (1694) with the somewhat elegiac remark which I placed at the beginning of this book:

'I see many who delight in mathematical doctrines turning away from metaphysics with abhorrence, for in the one they see light, in the other darkness' (GP IV, 468)

and on 13 March 1699 he writes to Malebranche that those who wish to think accurately and clearly should not turn their attention to mathematics alone but should consider metaphysics as well (GP I, 356).

Leibniz had some great predecessors in joining mathematics with metaphysics the first and greatest of whom is, of course, Plato, but there were others more or less immediately before his eyes such as Descartes, Galileo and Kepler. It is not surprising that Leibniz not only referred constantly to Plato as a decisive philosophical influence upon him, but also mentioned the three moderns as being of decisive importance for him (GP II, 288). It would not be proper to mention these names without also mentioning Whitehead who, in our own day, has realised anew this dual attitude to mathematics and metaphysics.

As a young man and as a student Leibniz's attention was mainly occupied by metaphysics. Not only do his first works bear witness to this, the *Disputatio de principio individui* (1663), the *Confessio naturae contra atheistas* (1668), the *Dissertatio de stylo Nizolii* (1770), but also a whole series of biographical notes. There is a not very deep interest in mathematics in the *De arte combinatoria*. The years which he spent in Paris were the time of his greatest mathematical and scientific interest and the period of his great discoveries, but his relations with Spinoza, Arnauld and Malebranche show clearly that even at this time Leibniz did not neglect the study of metaphysics. In his later years Leibniz renewed his study of metaphysics with great intensity, but this may be related to the reduction of his mathematical productivity, which is usually a gift of youth. Leibniz frequently states in his letters to Bernoulli that he now regards himself only as an onlooker, but one with specialised knowledge (GM III, 57, 99).

Leibniz was educated in the tradition of Aristotle and the scholastics by his teachers, Thomasius and Scherzer, even if the philosophy which they taught was a *philosophia reformata*. Although there is a lack of monographs on the subject we may assume that Leibniz constantly studied the original works of Plato, Aristotle, Thomas Aquinas, Duns Scotus and Suarez, but it is remarkable that the works of William of Ockham seemed to have attracted little attention from him, and Leibniz does not seem to have read him in the original texts. With this one exception Leibniz preserves the continuity of this great complex of philosophical thought and in support of it he is constantly defending metaphysics as the central philosophical task, for example in the eighth chapter of the fourth book of the *Nouveaux Essais*.

Leibniz takes over from Aristotle the double task of metaphysics: metaphysics is the doctrine of the *ens qua ens* and is at the same time the doctrine of the *ens primum*. We have distinguished between these two tasks as *metaphysica generalis* and *theologia naturalis* and developed them separately in the two preceding chapters. The task of metaphysics as *metaphysica generalis* is stated in *De arte combinatoria*: 'Metaphysics . . . is concerned with the *ens* and with the affections of the *ens*' (GP IV, 35). There is a similar statement in the *Nouveaux Essais*: 'metaphysics is the science of being in general '(GP V, 412). In Chapter III of Book IV the task of metaphysics in this respect is expanded:

'What is there that is more important, assuming that it is true, than that which we have determined about the nature of substances, about unities and pluralities, about singularity and plurality, about the inner constitution of individuals, about the impossibility of the vacuum and atoms, about the origin of cohesion, about the law of continuity and other natural laws, especially about the harmony of things, the immateriality of souls and bodies, the preservation of souls, even those of animals, beyond death. In all this there is nothing which I do not consider proved or able to be proved.'

Metaphysics as *theologia naturalis* is the subject of the *Theodicy*:

'. . . this superior science should have as its object being, and thus God as the source of being. M. Dreier of Königsberg has observed that the true metaphysics which Aristotle was seeking and which he called τὴν ἐητουμένην, his desideratum, was theology' (§ 104).

The most difficult problem in Leibnizian metaphysics is that of method, for he knows only one scientific method which is at the same time the mathematical and the metaphysical method. In this Leibniz is very strongly influenced by Descartes and Spinoza. However much he contradicts them he never contrived to free himself from their ideal of the use of mathematical method in metaphysics. This may be understandable in view of Leibniz's contribution to the creation of modern mathematics but it remains one of the weakest points of his metaphysics.

Leibniz constantly demands that philosophy and especially metaphysics, both as *metaphysica generalis* and *theologia naturalis*, should be developed to the same precision as mathematics (GP IV, 468, 471). Under the presuppositions of Leibniz's theory of science, this demand falls into two parts: the task of achieving exact definitions and the task of producing exact proofs.

The main failing of metaphysics, says Leibniz, is that it does not have exact definitions and in the *Meditationes* (1684) he gives metaphysical concepts as examples of obscure concepts (*notio obscura*), the concept of entelechy and the concept of cause. These concepts are so badly defined that they are not even unambiguous enough to be identified with certainty (GP IV, 422). In *De primae philosophiae emendatione et de notione substantiae* which appeared in the *Acta Eruditorum* (1694) Leibniz makes the same complaint:

'. . . the true and fruitful notions not only of substance, but of cause, action, relation, similarity and of many other terms are generally obscure' (GP IV, 468).

N

The uncertainty of metaphysical definitions must infect metaphysical proofs. The Greeks discovered the art of proof in mathematics, but made no use of it in philosophy, and so neither in Plato nor Aristotle are there really valid proofs, apart from Aristotelian logic (GP V, 352).

The vagueness of metaphysical definitions and proofs is particularly evident in *theologia naturalis*, but they are blemishes which can be cured and mathematics affords the model. Leibniz himself had made important discoveries along these lines; one day, and here we see Leibniz's optimism breaking through, metaphysics will consist, both as *theologia naturalis* and *metaphysica generalis*, of exact and unexceptionable proofs.

§ 41. A CRITIQUE OF LEIBNIZ'S METAPHYSICS

An exposé, we must reiterate, is itself an evaluation, but it may be of value to restate the evaluation once more.

In my opinion there are serious objections to regarding metaphysics as a science of definition and proof like mathematics. It is true that this is the very reason for Heinrich Scholz's high regard for Leibniz's metaphysics and his *Metaphysik im strengen Sinne* takes over Leibniz's ideal both in its title and in its method, but we are entitled to ask, both in the case of Leibniz and of Scholz, whether either of them has really achieved this mathematically, logically accurate metaphysics, even in an approximation, and ask further whether such an ideal is capable of being achieved at all.

In 1763 the Berlin Academy of Sciences made this the subject of a prize essay. It asked: 'Are metaphysical truths of the same evidence as mathematical?' Among the contestants were Kant and Mendelssohn, both of whom answered the question in the negative. We distinguish again between metaphysics as *metaphysica generalis* and metaphysics as *theologia naturalis*.

Can *theologia naturalis* achieve the same accuracy as logic and mathematics? We believe that the answer is 'No'. This view is supported by an expert monograph published in 1933 by Joseph Iwanicki, who is essentially well disposed towards Leibniz, entitled *Leibniz et les démonstrations mathématiques de l'existence de*

Dieu. Iwanicki, who believes that a *theologia naturalis* as such is a possibility, reaches the conclusion, after examining Leibniz's arguments, that the ideal of a *theologia naturalis* based on logic and mathematics cannot be regarded as a possible one and that this confirms the position of Thomas Aquinas.

'This is why St. Thomas concludes it is not possible to apply mathematical method to the knowledge of God: "they sin who strive to proceed uniformly". St. Thomas, Abicht, Mendelssohn and Kant are incontestably right: the Leibnizian ideal is utopian and the promise of rigorous geometrical proofs of God and mind will always remain unrealised' (p. 309).

Metaphysics as *metaphysica generalis* is also incapable of being elevated to a discipline of logical and mathematical exactitude. All experience of metaphysics as a scientific discipline from the time of Aristotle onwards argues against this, as does a sober observation of Leibniz's own results. It is only necessary to compare one of Leibniz's mathematical theories with one of his metaphysical theories in order to see how great is the difference between the methodological possibilities. If we compare, say, the representation of $\pi/4$ by the infinite series:

$$\pi/4 = 1 - \tfrac{1}{3} + \tfrac{1}{5} - \tfrac{1}{7} \ldots$$

which is one of Leibniz's great mathematical discoveries, with the doctrine of pre-established harmony, one of the fundamental theories of Leibnizian metaphysics, the difference is obvious at once. For this reason it is not possible to consider the achievement of a logically and mathematically exact metaphysics as a genuine goal.

It is possible, however, to agree completely with the notion that the being of the individual is true being. Perhaps we should subject the concept of what is alive to a closer consideration, but however we regard this idea, whether purely systematically, whether from the point of view of the analysis of meaning, whether positively or negatively, from every point of view it appears sufficient and well-founded. Systematically, the individual living being is what is truly real; epistemologically, the meaning of being is given by the being of the individual living being; positively, the individual living being is the bearer of all other being. Negatively, every other being, accidents, modifications, relations, universals, abstracts and all the others, when compared with the being of the individual living being has a lesser being. This was Aristotle's fundamental theory achieved in a profound argument with the doctrine of ideas, an argument which Plato himself had begun in his later dialogues. Thus the fundamental theory of the doctrine of monads, that the being of the individual, or in Leibnizian terms, the monad, represents true being, is the well-founded and well-preserved heritage of Aristotle in the philosophy of Leibniz.

On the other hand there seem to be many objections to Leibniz's doctrine of truth. He maintains the objectivity of truth, and explains this objectivity by saying that truth is understood as divine thought.

In this explanation of truth as divine thought we have to take note of objections both from the theological and the philosophical side. These focus on the question whether mathematics, as we know it, contains essential moments which are specific to human thought. We are concerned here with the problems of intuition, signs and discursiveness and the question is, if they are intrinsic to mathematics, can the difference between human and divine thought be justifiably regarded as of no consequence. In my view Leibniz was much too optimistic about this.

On the fundamental objectivity of truth, I believe that although many difficulties can be found in the manner in which Leibniz argues his case, nevertheless the case is fundamentally correct. If we regard logic and mathematics without bias then we cannot but recognise that, as Leibniz puts it, the Italians, the French and the Germans all have the same mathematics. Leibniz would probably, today, have expressed this in more general terms: in any case, the universal validity of mathematics is a fact and a singular phenomenon.

The objectivity of logical and mathematical truths, or in a more generalised form the objectivity of all truths, is merely another way of saying that these truths are universally valid; and this is clearly the case. Even this has been denied, but to deny so evident a phenomenon one must be blinded by prejudice.

It is, however, another problem altogether that there are such great, in fact almost insurmountable, difficulties in the interpretation of the objectivity of truth. Plato's doctrine of ideas is the first great attempt to get to grips with this problem and it was Plato who saw what difficulties were involved in a naïve doctrine of ideas. We may say that Aristotle is fundamentally occupied with the deepening of this interpretation of the objectivity of truth, and we may say that Thomas Aquinas tried to extend the relationship between Aristotle and Plato. This was Leibniz's own desire. Perhaps Leibniz was specially attracted to the doctrine of ideas, often in a very naïve version. Even so, it is a genuine problem, it is indeed the true problem of metaphysics. On the Aristotelian basis that true being is the being of the individual living being, or in Leibnizian terms, the being of the individual monad, an understanding of the objectivity of truth is the aim, which means historically an understanding of Plato. It is in this methodological goal that the true significance of Leibniz is to be sought.

NOTES

1. H. Scholz, *Leibniz und die mathematische Grundlagenforschung*. Jahresbericht der Deutschen Mathematiker Vereinigung, **52** (1942), 217 ff.

2. B. Russell, *A critical exposition of the philosophy of Leibniz*, 4th edn., London, 1951. Compare also: D. Mahnke, *Leibnizens Synthese von Universalmathematik und Individualmetaphysik*, Halle, 1926, § 6, and G. Bergmann, *Russell's examination of Leibniz examined*. Philosophy of science, **23** (1956), 175–203.

3. Leibniz's logic see I. M. Bochenski, *Formale Logik*, Freiburg, 1956, pp. 320 f., with a bibliography on pp. 585 ff.; K. Dürr, *Die mathematische Logik von Leibniz*. Studia Philosophica, **7** (1947), 87 ff.

4. L. Couturat, *Opuscules et fragments inédits de Leibniz*, Paris, 1903.

5. C. Hartshorne, *Leibniz's greatest discovery*. Journal of the History of Ideas, **7** (1946), 413.

6. *The Leibniz-Clarke Correspondence*. Edited by H. G. Alexander, Manchester, 1956.

7. H. Herring, *Leibniz' principium identitatis indiscernibilium und die Leibniz-Kritik Kants*. Kant-Studien, **49** (1957/8), 389 ff.

8. R. Whittemore, *Dogma and sufficient reason in the cosmology of Leibniz*. Tulane studies in Philosophy, New Orleans, 1952. R. Zocher, *Zum Satz vom zureichenden Grunde bei Leibniz*. Beiträge zur Leibnizforschung ed. Schischkoff, Reutlingen, 1947, pp. 68 f. C. Giacon, *La causalita nel rationalismo moderno*, Milan, 1954. S. del Boca, *Finalismo e necessita in Leibniz* and *Meccanismo e finalita in Leibniz*, both Florence, 1936.

9. A. Becker, *Bestreitet Aristoteles die Gültigkeit des tertium non datur für Zukunfts-aussagen?* Actes du congrès internat. de philosophie scientifique, Paris, 1936, VI, 69 ff.

10. N. Hartmann, *Möglichkeit und Wirklichkeit*, Berlin, 1938, p. 45 f.

11. Ref. 1, p. 228.

12. H. Scholz, *Metaphysik als strenge Wissenschaft*, Cologne, 1941, p. 47.

13. L. Couturat, ref. 4, pp. 356 ff. and *La Logique de Leibniz*, Paris, 1901, chapter VI, § 12. See also Mahnke, ref. 2, § 7, and A. Korcik, *Couturat's method of solving the problem of Leibniz concerning the number of subjects and predicates in a proposition*. Roczniki filozoficzne, **4** (1954), 86.

14. Couturat, *Logique* (ref. 13), p. 36 n. 2. R. Dalbiez, *L'idée fondamentale de la combinatoire leibnizienne*. Congrès Descartes, VI (1937), 3 ff.

15. Couturat, *Logique*, pp. 42 and 61.

16. Couturat, *Logique*, p. 194, and further passages given in note 3. M. Guéroult, *Substance and the primitive simple notion in the philosophy of Leibniz*. Philosophy and Phenomenological Research, **7** (1947), pp. 293 ff. G. Grua, *Jurisprudence universelle et Théodicée selon Leibniz*, Paris, 1953, II, pp. 274 ff.

17. Couturat, *Logique*, p. 210; Russell, *Leibniz*, p. 17.

18. *Discours de métaphysique*, § 8, GP IV, 433, and Couturat, *Logique*, p. 208 n. 2.

19. Couturat, *Logique*, pp. 8 ff. and 443 ff.

20. K. Dürr, *Neue Beleuchtung einer Theorie von Leibniz*, Darmstadt, 1930.

21. Couturat, *Logique*, pp. 389 ff.

22. C. Prantl, *Geschichte der Logik im Abendlande*, Leipzig, 1855, Vol. I, pp. 286 f.

23. J. Hofmann, *Die Entwicklungsgeschichte der Leibnizschen Mathematik*, Munich, 1949.

24. Russell, *Leibniz*, p. 6. G. Cantelli, *La disputa Leibniz-Newton sull'analisi. Scelta da documenti degli anni 1672-1716*, Turin, 1958. J. O. Fleckenstein, *Der Prioritätsstreit zwischen Leibniz und Newton*, Basel, 1956.

25. K. Dürr, *Leibniz' Forschungen im Gebiet der Syllogistik*. Leibniz zu seinem 300. Geburtstage, Berlin, 1949, Lieferung 5; also *Neue Beleuchtung einer Theorie von Leibniz*, Darmstadt, 1930. R. M. Yost, *Leibniz and philosophical analysis*, Berkeley, 1954. H. Scholz, *Geschichte der Logik*, Berlin, 1931, pp. 48 ff. I. M. Bochenski, *Formale Logik*, Freiburg, 1956, pp. 301 f.

26. H. Weyl, *Die heutige Erkenntnislage der Mathematik*. Symposion, 1 (1925), 30. H. L. Matzat, *Untersuchungen über die metaphysischen Grundlagen der Leibnizchen Zeichenkunst*, Berlin, 1938.

27. Couturat, *Inédits*, pp. 191, 219, 516.

28. W. Kabitz, *Die Philosophie des jungen Leibniz*, Heidelberg, 1909.

29. D. Hilbert, *Grundlagen der Geometrie*, 4th edn., Leipzig, 1913, p. 25.

30. K. Huber, *Leibniz*, München, 1951, pp. 370 f. G. Martin, *Existenz und Widerspruchsfreiheit in der Logik von Leibniz*. Kant-Studien, 48 (1956/57), 202 ff.

31. L. Lomker, *Leibniz's Doctrine of Ideas*. The Philosophical Review, 55 (1946), pp. 229 ff. E. Colorni, *La verità eterne in Descartes e in Leibniz*. Congrès Descartes, I, 1937, pp. 132 ff.

32. A Robinet, *Malebranche et Leibniz*, Paris, 1955.

33. B. Bolzano, *Wissenschaftslehre*, I, Leipzig, 1914, pp. 113 f.

34. Ref. 25, p. 40.

35. Ref. 12, p. 140.

36. Hegel, *Vorlesungen über die Geschichte der Philosophie*. Works ed. Glockner, XIX, 461.

37. W. Cramer, *Das Absolute und das Kontingente*, Frankfurt, 1959. Chapter V. Die Einheit der Substanz. Leibniz' Monadologie.

38. A. Foucher de Careil, *Nouvelles lettres et opuscules inédits de Leibniz*, Paris, 1857, pp. 44–145; *Discours de Metaphysique*, § 20. P. Burgelin, *Commentaire du Discours de Metaphysique de Leibniz*, Paris, 1959, p. 222. J. Politella, *Platonism, Aristotelianism and Cabalism in the Philosophy of Leibniz*, Philadelphia, 1938.

39. G. Martin, *Wilhelm von Ockham*, Berlin, 1949, § 4–§ 7.

40. D. Nolen, *Quid Leibnitius Aristoteli debuerit*, Paris, 1875, p. 25. L. Stein, *Leibniz und Spinoza*, Berlin, 1890, pp. 148 ff. Thomas Aquinas, *De potentia*, q. 9 a. 1 ad 4. Suarez, *Disputationes metaphysicae*, XXXIII, 2, 18. *Works*, XXVI, 345. L. Pelloux, *Leibniz e Aristotele*. Revista di Filosofia Neo-Scolastica, 39 (1947), 285. O. Hamelin, *Sur ce que Leibniz doit à Aristote*. Les Etudes Philosophiques, 12 (1957), 139. G. Grua, *La position de Leibniz par rapport aux ontologies scolastiques et ses conséquences dans sa doctrine*. Doctor communis, 4 (1951), 102 ff. M. Wundt, *Die geschichtlichen Grundlagen von Leibniz' Metaphysik*. Zeitschrift für philosophische Forschung, 11 (1957), 497. J. Christensen, *A note concerning the Scholastic background of Leibniz's philosophy*. Theoria, 19 (1953), 172.

41. W. Werckmeister, *Der Leibnizsche Substanzbegriff*, Halle, 1899, p. 21.

J. Jalabert, *La théorie leibnizienne de la substance*, Paris, 1947. R. Pavese, *Il concetto die sostanza in Leibniz e la sua integrazione*. Sophia, **6** (1938), 313.

42. G. Martin, *Der Begriff der Realität bei Leibniz*. Kant-Studien, **49** (1957), (58), 82. J. O. Fleckenstein, *G. W. Leibniz*, München, 1958, p. 117. F. H. Jacobi, *Werke*, II, 2, Leipzig, 1819, pp. 97 ff. Schelling, *Ideen zu einer Philosophie der Natur*. Works ed. Schröter, München, 1927, I, 687. H. H. Holz, *Schelling über Leibniz*. Deutsche Zeitschrift für Philosophie, **2** (1954), 755. Hegel, *Vorlesungen über die Geschichte der Philosophie*. Works ed. Glockner, XIX, 449. J. Heimsoeth, *Die Methode der Erkenntnis bei Descartes und Leibniz*, Giessen, 1914, p. 275. W. Kabitz, *Die Philosophie des jungen Leibniz*, Heidelberg, 1909, p. 4. H. Schmalenbach, *Leibniz*, München, 1921 passim, 206 ff. D. Mahnke, *Leibnizens Synthese*, Halle, 1925, Chapters IV and V. H. W. B. Joseph, *Lectures on the Philosophy of Leibniz*, Oxford, 1949. A. Cresson, *Leibniz, sa vie, son œuvre, sa philosophie*, Paris, 1958. J. Moreau, *L'univers leibnizien*, Lyon, 1956. C. Ottaviano, *Le basi fisico-metafisiche della filosofia di Leibniz*, Padua, 1952. S. del Boca, *Leibniz*, Milan, 1947. N. Hartmann, *Leibniz als Metaphysiker*. Leibniz zu zeinem 300. Geburtstag. Berlin, 1946, I.

43. F. S. C. Northrop, *Leibniz's Theory of Space*. Journal of the History of Ideas, **7** (1946), 422. E. Cassirer, *Newton and Leibniz*. The Philosophical Review, **52** (1943). R. Wavre, *L'espace pour Leibniz*. Studia Philosophica, **7** (1947), 245. C. D. Broad, *Leibniz's last controversy with the Newtonians*. Theoria, **12** (1946), 143.

44. K. Hildebrandt, *Leibniz und das Reich der Gnade*. The Hague, 1953.

45. E. Cassirer, *Leibniz' System in seinen wissenschaftlichen Grundlagen*, Marburg, 1902.

46. L. J. Russell, *Leibniz's account of phenomena*. Proceedings of the Aristotelian Society, **54** (1953), 167. N. Rescher, *Leibniz's conception of quantity, number and infinity*. The Philosophical Review, **64** (1955), 108.

AUTHOR INDEX

(For Leibniz's correspondents, see index of Leibniz's Works under 'Correspondence with . . .')

INDEX OF LEIBNIZ'S WORKS